MW00587269

The Study Skills Handbook:

How to Ace Tests, Get Straight A's, and Succeed in School

By Peter Hollins,
Author and Researcher at
petehollins.com

Table of Contents

Chapter 1. Making the Most of Classroom Time

Whether you're a school or university student or an adult learner, and no matter the subject you're tackling, you obviously appreciate the value of learning. But if you've picked up this book, you also understand that there's value in a kind of meta-learning, i.e. *learning how to learn*.

Isn't it strange how many of us simply take for granted the processes by which we learn new information? Maybe we think that good intentions, a bit of intelligence, and enough hard work are all it takes to succeed at our chosen study. While nobody would argue you don't need these things, the truth is that becoming good at learning seldom happens by accident—we need to have a proven, practical strategy for exactly **how** we're going to get the most out of the study process.

This is what this book is about. We're going to cover all those study skills that you weren't taught at school but should have been. There will be a few familiar ideas in the chapters that follow (like how best to tackle tests, boost your memory, or draw up a study plan), but be prepared for a few unexpected ideas, too. The best thing is that even once you're done studying or aced your tests, the approaches and techniques that you learn here will continue to be useful to you all throughout life.

Let's start in the most obvious place: the classroom. One of the greatest study skills you could hope to master is *listening*. You've heard it all before, but listening is not a passive process, and it's definitely not the same as merely hearing. If up until now you've simply turned up to classes or lectures and sat down without a plan, well, you've been missing out. Listening is really a multi-stage process in which we receive, digest, and respond to the information that we hear.

So, how do you become a better listener? Well, that depends on how well you're currently absorbing and processing information at each level.

Practicing Effective Listening During Class

For our purposes, we can imagine that there are five stages in the listening process. Rather than sitting in the classroom and hoping that some knowledge will somehow magically float over to us, we have to see ourselves as engaged and aware information *receptors*.

The Reception Stage
Physiologically, the organs in your inner ear may be registering the sound waves and transmitting the information to your brain, but it all "goes in one ear and out the other" unless one crucial ingredient is present: your attention.

Your attention is what focuses your perception and shapes what you're perceiving into meaningful data that you can then store and remember. Often, when people think they have poor memories, the problem is that they never really attended in the first place. We'll go more into the neuroscience details of learning later on, but for now, improving the receiving stage comes down to eliminating as many distractions and disruptions as possible, i.e. anything that threatens to interrupt your attention.

The Understanding Stage
What do the words you're hearing actually *mean*?

Comprehension happens continually in the listening process as the brain works hard to interpret context, infer meanings, and put together all the separate pieces of information into a coherent narrative they can actually do something with. Once you know the point the speaker is trying to make, you can frame and predict what else is said and see the bigger picture. Have you ever had the experience of hearing what someone said, understanding the individual words and sentences, but somehow still having zero clue what any of it meant or what larger framework it fit into? You were probably having difficulties at this stage!

We need to know the who, what, where, and, most importantly, why. We need to know not just the details of the message, but the purpose of it being communicated and what we're supposed to do with that information. The best way to do this in the moment is to ask questions. As you're constructing your own mental representation of the speaker's argument, you can actively seek to fill in any holes— learning is always best when teacher and learner can engage in a reciprocal dialogue.

The Evaluating Stage
You're not just a sponge; you have opinions. You assess and evaluate what you hear, which is the first stage of producing your own original response to it. Evaluations can be done on many levels—you can decide whether you agree or not, how well you think the argument itself has been made, whether you find the information significant to your life, or what you think about any biases or falsehoods in the

content or delivery. You can also evaluate how well you've absorbed the material and what's still unclear for you.

As you listen, you're actively fitting in the new data alongside all the banked knowledge and understanding you already have—and possibly noticing any discrepancies or confirmations.

The Responding Stage
Once you've done this, it's natural to have a reaction to what you've heard, and that includes thoughts, feelings, behaviors, or communication, both verbal and nonverbal. You could ask a question to deliberately guide the direction of the conversation or lesson, you could nod and smile, you could quietly decide you're not going to pay attention anymore, or you could actively take notes, adding in your own observations.

The Remembering Stage
You can't really be said to have learned something unless you are able to file it away well enough in your memory so that it can be retrieved again later. Memory is like

a computer filing system—the more clearly and deliberately you organize and tag your memories, the easier it will be to find and recall them later.

But you're actively using your memory even while you're listening, too. We use memory to fill in gaps as we listen, to retain information from the beginning of the lesson or even sentence, and to draw on what we already know to help us better comprehend the new material. Context doesn't just expand outward in the present moment, but reaches back into the past. It's only by using our memory that we can make logical connections and causal links, gaining proper insight into what we're being told. This means that the solidity of what we've already remembered from previous lessons actively influences how well we're learning and remembering the *current* lesson.

So, these are the five stages of listening. In reality, the stages overlap and repeat continually as we listen. But, if there are issues with any one aspect, it's bound to interfere with your overall listening—and reduce how much you're learning and retaining. If you're just pitching up to lessons with no plan and no structure to shape and focus your listening, you're not going to be reaching your full potential.

In the next section, we'll be looking at concrete study techniques, but none of them will work as well as they could without solid listening skills to support them. When you understand that learning is a cycle or a coordination of many different capacities and processes, then you can design an approach that will actually get you the results you want from the moment you sit down to start your lesson. Picture listening as occurring on a continuum—we could all stand to learn not exactly to listen more, but to practice *better quality* listening.

The HEAR Technique

This anagram (which is helpfully "hear") is something to quickly remember during lessons to help you focus attention and *really* listen.

H is for HALT—stop everything else you're doing and consciously decide to focus all your awareness on the important thing: the new material unfolding in front of you. Turn off your phone, quieten down your inner talk, and stop multitasking. Cutting out distractions in the moment is great, but this also extends to good preparation, i.e. making sure you have secured enough dedicated time to study and study alone, where you know you won't be interrupted.

E is for ENGAGE—now take all that brain power and put it on the speaker/lecturer/teacher. Depending on the kind of study you're doing, you can take notes, ask questions, respond with feedback, make mind maps, or record your own reactions or objections. If you can, steer the lesson or bring your own knowledge into the mix. Summarize, paraphrase, and draw connections. Think of it as a dialogue, i.e. you and the new material are having a conversation together.

A is for ANTICIPATE—you don't have to just sit and wait patiently to see what information will be sent your way. Predict what will come next—this will greatly increase your comprehension and recall and give you a richer grasp on the material. Ask yourself questions and see if the unfolding information is answering them. Be your own inner teacher as you prompt yourself with cues and questions. This will help you draw a connecting thread through the content, as well as keep you interested and focused.

R is for REPLAY—no, this is not for the day after or for months later when you start studying for a test! Replay is best done in the moment as you're engaging with the material. Think about what you're hearing and repeat it or write it down in your own words. Extract the key ideas of every sentence as you hear it. You might like to simply replay the overall theme or structure of the lesson to recap.

Now, the above looks easy and straightforward, and it is. But it *does* take practice to make a long-lasting habit. You already know that in your studies, it takes time to grasp new ideas and to make them automatic—listening is no different. This is especially true if you've spent literally your whole life doing "passive" listening or studying with zero plan or strategy.

Notetaking

Let's return to that second part of the HEAR anagram—engage. Taking notes is an obvious way to engage with the material, but it's sadly an activity that is subject to becoming automatic and meaningless. Have you ever just mindlessly jotted down a few phrases you heard and then promptly forgot about it all, never to look at those notes ever again? It's not that taking notes is useless; it's just that it matters a lot *how* you take those notes—intention, strategy, and focused awareness make all the difference. Your notes need to **transform** what you're hearing, not just passively record it.

One powerful method of transforming information is the Peter method. The origin? Well, me! Suffice to say, I have researched and studied the process of learning for years, and am familiar with all the existing models for notetaking out there. This method combines the best of what I've found in a system that I believe is the most thorough and helpful.

The Peter method uses four steps to take notes that lead to a deep understanding of your subject of study. The Peter method does require more work than normal notetaking, but that's part of what makes it more effective. (Sorry, there were never going to be any shortcuts in this book, just smarter approaches.)

Instead of allowing notetaking to be a brief, mostly passive exercise, the Peter method forces you to highlight the key points in your subject and compels you to extract the salient information for yourself in your own words. It enables you to process and elaborate upon the information you're studying in a reliable, systematic way, which makes learning and retaining the information you study infinitely easier.

The four steps are: (1) normal notetaking with as much detail as you can, (2) summarizing the information in your own words and clarifying the significance and noting questions, (3) connecting this particular piece of information to the lesson at large, and then (4) answering remaining questions and then summarizing each distinct page or section again.

The first step of the Peter method is to take notes as you ordinarily would. Copy down the information you need to know as you encounter the material, **but leave two blank lines beneath each note you take**. These lines give you space to process and analyze the information in the second and third steps. For maximum retention, it's best to engage in these later steps immediately after you finish your class, video, or reading. So the first step is to simply carry on as you normally would in as much detail as you can.

For example, if you were researching the diet of King Henry VIII, you might write (the following is all fabricated information for the purpose of illustration), "King Henry and his court consumed up to twenty different types of meat in one sitting. Serving less was considered an insult to nobles of the time. Vegetables and wine were also served, but the focus was on the meat, as it was considered a sign of wealth and status."

Step two: once you've taken your initial notes, move on to what really differentiates the Peter method from other forms of notetaking. It starts on the second line for each note, where you left space, and you summarize what you wrote in step one in a complete sentence. When you do this, it's important not to just repeat the initial note, even if you took your notes in complete sentences. Using your own words, converting the note to language that helps you understand the meaning of the note is essential. Ideally, you are able to abstract a deeper level of understanding. Really seek to make connections and find relationships within the information.

This isn't applicable to every piece of information, but do it anyway. Why? While it can seem redundant, the repetition itself also helps to cement the knowledge in your mind. The emphasis on repeating the knowledge in your own words, and in a fully coherent, complete sentence, requires you to process the information natively and chew on its meaning, making the information entrench itself in your mind more deeply than it would for a facile repetition.

When rephrasing the information from our example above, you might write, "Henry VIII's diet was mainly meat. In those years, rich and noble people expected a lot of different meats and felt insulted when offered too little variety. Wine and vegetables didn't matter much."

On the second line of your notes, you can also list any questions you have about the notes you took in step one. These are points of clarification, or gaps in your knowledge, that you feel you would need to form a complete picture. Before you move on to the next step of the Peter method, consider the directions this information might lead and what that all means. Whether you can or cannot answer it, considering the subject deeply enough to form a question will help you remember the facts.

Questions you might have about Henry VIII's diet are, "What were the health effects with such a protein-rich diet?" or, "How many people were involved in getting that much meat on a daily basis, and how did they do it?" or, "What did peasants eat by contrast?" or, "What did other nobles from other cultures or countries consider high status?"

Use a highlighter or a different-colored pen or pencil to make this section stand out, as this is the actual information and message you've extracted from the brain dump of the first step. It's actually unlikely that you'll ever refer back to what you produced in the first step.

Step three: in the third line, the final blank line you left for yourself, state any connections you can find between the subject of that note and the broader topic you're studying. If you notice that the topic of your note has some sort of cause-and-effect relationship with the broader topic, write that here. If this new information helps understand the motivating factors or connects events or allows you to guess at people's perspective/perceptions, write those here too. Anything you can do to form lateral connections to related information should be written down here so that the links—and thus the original information—can become consistent residents of your memory banks.

The rule of thumb is to simply ask how it fits in and why it matters. Following our example, suppose the greater lesson is about Henry VIII's life and legacy. Why does information about his diet and eating habits matter?

So here you might note that the royal's diet contrasted dramatically with peasant diets, which were largely composed of fruits, vegetables, and hearty grains they farmed themselves. Perhaps this led to Henry's subjects hating and eventually executing him. You might also note that such ample, stately meals likely contributed to Henry VIII's well-known obesity. Finally, you might also see the connection that this type of opulence was a sign of how absurdly rich the nobility was at the time. Or perhaps it was just an interesting anecdote on his opulence.

Find how the information contributes to an overall narrative or story. See it as a living and breathing factor instead of a dry factoid.

Step four: the final step of the Peter method is to take a break every page (or applicable chunk) to write a summary of the information from your second and third steps. Also make sure to try to address the questions you wrote in the second step if they are still applicable.

The final step creates a fourth opportunity for you to revisit, synthesize, and transform the information you're learning on paper. If most people review information once, then you've done it four times in four different ways. To say this is helpful would be an understatement. The mental work will go a long way to making sure you truly understand and remember the facts you're learning and the implications of that information. This doesn't only help you comprehend the information but will help you apply and manipulate that information if necessary.

To finish up your notes on Henry VIII's diet, you write, "Henry VIII's court expected to consume twenty types of meat with each meal. This consumption of meat was unusual at the time, as most couldn't afford much meat at all and consumed only fruits, vegetables, and grain they could raise themselves. This may be why Henry VIII and people who ate as he did were obese. I wonder how they got so much meat, and what other health effects resulted from this diet? What effect did this type of spending have on his people's perception of him?"

As you can see, the Peter method pays notetaking the respect and attention it deserves. When we take notes, we are not just recording information; we are creating the mental blueprint for how we perceive and understand this information for all time. This is our chance at making an accurate and deeply comprehensive first impression, so we can't spoil it with normal notes. The method leads to a much deeper, much better integrated knowledge set—

and that's exactly what makes information stick. If you want to remember and understand what you learn, the Peter method is the best method.

Mind Maps

Another great method for processing, organizing, and *engaging* with the new material coming your way is mind mapping. But again, this is a technique that needs to be done consciously and with a focused strategy—too many students out there have sat down to scribble out the mind map they believe they should generate, but only end up wasting their time since the exercise does precisely zero for their understanding.

Mind mapping is an invaluable technique that will help you organize the concepts, descriptions, and connections you discover between various topics in a manner that is both simple and easy to remember. But you need to do it right. Remember, your goal is not simply to generate a nice-looking page of notes or diagrams. It's to *use these in the aid of your understanding*. If they don't add to understanding, they're just a distraction.

Mind maps will also help give direction to your study since it makes it easier to know what you've covered already, how it all connects to each other, and which areas you need to know more about. It's in the name: you need to create a physical "map" of what's in your mind, thereby cementing and organizing it clearly for yourself.

While there are several ways of illustrating your thoughts and work, such as concept webs, spider diagrams, and others, mind mapping has several unique benefits to offer. It allows you to see the bigger picture because of the way mind maps are constructed, thus letting you stay focused on the important parts without getting sidetracked.

The colorful nature of mind maps also helps you retain more of the information you put down in them. Lastly, when studying complex topics, you can use several mind maps to efficiently break down and summarize different subtopics while keeping your material brief and uncluttered.

How to Make a Mind Map

Tony Buzan, the creator of mind maps, has some guidelines on how to effectively make mind maps. All you need for this exercise are some sheets of paper and at least three different colored pens or pencils.

Step 1

Start by placing the sheet of paper horizontally in front of you, zeroing in on the center of the page. You can either use an image related to your main topic or draw a circle and write it within that. Generally, it is a good idea to use symbols, images, and drawings to represent information to facilitate better retention. However, words and bubbles will also do just fine.

Step 2

Draw thick branches that stick out of your central image or bubble in different directions. These can be called your main branches. Use your colored pens to create some contrast, and draw additional bubbles at the end of these branches. Write or draw major subtopics within these bubbles. For example, if you're studying philosophy, your branches can be about different subfields within philosophy, such as ethics, metaphysics, political philosophy, epistemology, etc.

Step 3

Continue making branches within your subtopics and ensure that they are spaced out enough to minimize clutter. So if your subtopic is ethics, you can go further and note schools of thought, such as utilitarianism and deontology. For political philosophy, you can have democracy, oligarchy, aristocracy, and tyranny as sub-fields.

Step 4

Keep drawing new branches that further specify the content of the bubbles they extend from. For example, for utilitarianism you can simply write "the greatest happiness of the greatest number," whereas deontology can be a "rules-based theory."

That's all you need to do. It's really this simple. Draw a circle in the center and keep making branches with more bubbles, which in turn have their own branches and bubbles, till you've filled up the entire sheet of paper. When tackling entire disciplines like philosophy or psychology, it might be helpful to make multiple mind maps. This would work exactly the same way, except the middle bubble would contain your sub-topic, such as political philosophy, instead of your larger area of interest. This will help you be more comprehensive in accumulating and organizing everything you've learned.

Here is another example of how you can make a mind map.

Step 1

Say you want to make a mind map about different political ideologies. You can write "political ideologies" in the central bubble and draw four branches from it.

Step 2

These branches end with their own bubbles, within which you can write liberalism, communism, anarchism, and fascism. Alternatively, you can use symbols to denote them. Use the Statue of Liberty for liberalism, the face of Karl Marx for communism, Mussolini for fascism, and the symbol of anarchism, which is a capital A with a circle around the middle.

Step 3

Within these, draw more branches and bubbles that extend from each of these subtopics. Fill in the relevant information through words or images. So liberalism can have the phrase "liberty, equality, fraternity" in one bubble, private property in another, free and fair elections in the third one, so on and so forth. Similarly, communism can have "state control over the economy," "classless society," "abolition of religion," etc.

Step 4

Continue the above process until you reach the end of your sheet of paper.

Let's consider one final example of how to create a mind map for your studies.

Step 1

Assume you want to draw a mind map to study US history. Write "US History" in a bubble around the middle of your paper and extend at least six branches from it. You can choose to use more depending on how extensively you're studying the topic, but for our purpose, six will suffice.

Step 2

At the end of these main branches, you can note down the major periods or landmark events. So you can start with the arrival of the Pilgrims at Plymouth Rock, proceeding to the American Revolution, and then the Civil War, US involvement in the World Wars, followed by the Cold War, and then lump the rest into post-1990 history.

Step 3

As before, extend branches from these subtopics within US history. For the first part, you may want to cover Thanksgiving, the Pilgrims' interaction with Native Americans, etc. Carry on with major events from the Revolution, like the Boston Tea Party, its various causes, the adoption of democracy as a form of rule, and so on. Similarly proceed with the Civil War, World Wars, and Cold War, along with their landmark events, notable incidents, outcomes, and statistics.

Step 4

Continue adding more depth to your points and include sufficient detail so you can come back to the map and still glean most of the relevant information pertaining to this topic.

Tips and Tricks to Improve Your Mind Maps

The most basic mind map can be made using just a pen or pencil and with bubbles and branches on paper. However, such a map is unlikely to be memorable, which is one of the key reasons for using mind mapping as a technique in the first place.

There are several things you can do to enhance your mind maps and maximize how useful they are in your efforts toward becoming a polymath. The following tips and tricks will help you in that endeavor:

1. Minimize the number of words you use. Keep the information inside your bubbles brief and to the point.
2. Maximize visual aids like colors, symbols, drawings, etc. You can also use written words in different ways. So one main branch from your central bubble can have text written only in lowercase, while another has text exclusively uppercase.
3. Emphasize certain words or parts of the text you've included in your map to exhibit their importance.
4. Make the main branches thicker, and gradually reduce the thickness as you proceed deeper into the mind map. This is another visual cue that will help you remember the hierarchy of your information.
5. Don't restrict yourself to bubbles; use different shapes at the end of your

main branches and for that entire part of your mind map. These shapes can help you differentiate the various parts of your map and recall them more clearly.

SQ3R

As you can see, these methods all have something important in common: they're about structure and deliberate organization. In a way, it doesn't matter how you engage and analyze material, only that you're actually doing it. The way you process and digest material depends on a lot of factors, including the subject.

One particular framework for getting the most out of a resource is called the SQ3R method, developed by American educator Francis P. Robinson. It's great for any material that you have to sift through primarily by reading (i.e. most of it!). It is named for its five components:

- survey

- question

- read

- recite

- review

Survey. The first step in the method is getting a general overview of what you'll be reading. Textbooks and nonfiction works aren't like fiction or narrative literature in which you just start from the beginning and wind your way through each chapter. The best works of nonfiction are arranged to impart information in a way that's clear and memorable and builds upon each previous chapter. If you dive in without surveying first, you are going in blind, without understanding where you are going and what you are trying to accomplish. You should get a lay of the land first *before* you delve into Chapter 1. The survey component enables you to get the most general introduction to the topic so you can establish and shape the goals you want to achieve from reading the book.

It's just like taking a look at the entire map before you set off on a road trip. You may not need all the knowledge at the moment, but understanding everything as a whole and how it fits together will help you with the small details and when you're in the weeds. You'll know that you generally need to head southwest if you're confused.

In the SQ3R method, surveying means examining the structure of the work: the book title, the introduction or preface, section titles, chapter titles, headings, and subheadings. If the book is illustrated with pictures or graphics, you'd review them. You could also make note of the conventions the book uses to guide your reading: typefaces, bold or italic text, and chapter objectives and study questions if they're in there. In using the survey step, you're setting up expectations for what you're going to be reading about, and giving yourself an initial framework to structure your goals for reading the material.

Beyond books, you should survey all the important concepts in a discipline. If you can't find it within a structure like a book's table of contents, then you need to be able to create it for yourself. Yes, this is the difficult part, but once you are able to lay all the concepts out and understand how they relate to each other at least on a surface level, you will already be leaps ahead of others. Use the survey component to form an outline of what you'll learn. In a sense, it's more like you're plotting out a metaphorical "book" for yourself.

In this phase, you'll want to determine exactly what you *want* to become knowledgeable about as specifically as you can. For example, if you want to learn all about psychology, that's going to take a significant amount of time. It won't happen in one shot. You'd want to specify it a little more: the early history of psychoanalysis, the works of Sigmund Freud and Carl Jung, sports psychology, developmental psychology—the possibilities are plentiful.

You'll want to keep an eye out for phrases or concepts that appear in several different sources since they represent elements that come up often in your chosen field and might be things you have to know. Draw connections and cause-and-effect relationships before even diving into any of the concepts in detail.

Question. In the second stage of the SQ3R method, you're still not diving into the deep end. During the question stage, you'll work a little more deeply to prepare your mind to focus and interact with the material you're reading. You'll take a slightly closer look at the structure of the book and form some questions you want answered, or set up the objectives you hope to achieve.

In the question phase of reading a book— or, more precisely at this point, *preparing* to read—you'd go through the chapter titles, headings, and subheadings and rephrase them in the form of a question. This turns the dry title the author has given into a challenge or problem for you to solve. For example, if you're reading a book on Freud, there might be a chapter called "Foundations of Freud's Analyses of Dreams." You'd rewrite this chapter title as "How did Sigmund Freud's work on dream interpretation originate, and what were his very first ideas on the subject?" You could pencil that question in the margin of your book. If you're reading a textbook with study questions at the ends of the chapters, those serve as excellent guides to what you're about to find out.

Now that you've organized your resources for study planning, you can arrange some of the topics you're going to cover into questions you want answered or objectives you want to meet. Based on the source material you've lined up and the patterns you might have observed, what specific answers are you hoping to find in your studies? Write them down. This is also a good time to come up with a structure for answering your questions—a daily journal, a self-administered quiz, some kind of "knowledge tracker"? You don't have to answer the questions yet—you just need to know how you're going to record them when you do.

Reading. In this stage, you're finally ready to dive into the material. Because you've gotten the lay of the land and formed some questions and goals for your studies, you're a little more engaged when you finally sit down to read. You're looking for answers to the questions you've raised. Another underrated aspect of formulating and organizing before you actually begin reading is to build *anticipation* for learning. You've been looking over everything for a while now, and you'll probably be eager to finally dive in and answer the questions you've been mentally accumulating.

This step is where most people try to start but fail because they lack a foundation and instead have unreasonable expectations.

Now you're being deliberate and paced about your reading so you can comprehend better. This means slowing down—a *lot.* Be patient with the material and with yourself. If a passage is difficult to understand, read it extremely slowly. If you aren't getting clarity about a certain part, stop, go back to the beginning, and reread it. It's not like you're reading a page-turner novel that you can't put down. You're reading information that might be densely packed—so tackle it slowly and attentively one section at a time.

Chances are that reading is part of your study plan, but so might be visual aids, online courses, and internet resources. Use them exactly the way you'd use the book in the reading phase: deliberately and persistently, with the goal of fully understanding each concept you're being taught. If you get lost, remember the rewind button and scrolling are your best buddies. Plan your study time around getting as complete a level of comprehensiveness as you can.

Reciting. This step is crucial in processing the information you're learning about and is the biggest difference between reading to learn and reading for entertainment. Now that you're familiar with the material, the aim of the reciting phase is to reorient your mind and attention to focus and learn more fully as you go along. In other words, this step is about literal recitation.

Ask questions—out loud, verbally—about what you're reading. This is also the point where you take copious notes in the margins of the text and underline or highlight key points. Recitation occurs verbally and also through writing. However, it's important to restate these points *in your own words* rather than to just copy phrases from the book onto a piece of paper. By doing this, you're taking the new knowledge and putting it into phrases you already know the meaning of. This makes the information easier to grasp in a language you understand. It makes it significant and meaningful to you.

If you have a geology book, you might rephrase and rewrite key points in the following way, starting from the original text:

> "This comparison suggests that the slow progress of erosion on hills and mountains is similar to the much more rapid and observable changes seen in miniature all around us."

You could rewrite the above into something like this:

> "Mountains and hills experience the same decay as happens in lowlands and rivers, just more slowly. Similar to baseball players."

What I'm doing here is putting one single bit of information into two distinct phrases, one of which I had to come up with myself. This is a huge tool that's used in memorization, and it's also a great way to make the information more meaningful to me personally. I also added a bit about baseball because I like baseball, and it makes the concept instantly understandable when I look back at it. Repeated throughout the course of a whole book, this process multiplies your learning capacity by itself.

The recitation phase in organizing your studies is great because it works across different mediums, and there are plenty of ways you can express your questions and restatements.

Review. The final stage of the SQ3R plan is when you go back over the material that you've studied, refamiliarize yourself with the most important points, and build your skills at memorizing the material.

Robinson breaks this stage down into specific days of the week, but we'll just mention some of the tactics in general. They include writing more questions about important parts you have highlighted, orally answering some of the questions if you can, reviewing your notes, creating flashcards for important concepts and terminology, rewriting the table of contents using your own words, and building out a mind map.

Any kind of practice that helps you drill down, take in, and commit information to memory is fair game (though flashcards are especially effective).

This step is meant to strengthen your memory of the material, but it does more than that. It can help you see connections and similarities between different aspects that you might not have picked up at first, and put concepts and ideas into greater context. It can also improve your mental organization skills so you can use this practice for other topics.

Think of this step as the natural continuation of the survey. At this point, you've gained an outline of the field, you've gotten into the nitty-gritty, and now you should take a step back, reevaluate, and make updated, more accurate, and insightful connections. Pair that with memorization, and your path to self-learning and expertise becomes essentially a shortcut. Flashcards. Mind maps. Timelines. Unanswered follow-up questions. Categorizing. Critical analysis, drawing conclusions, and asking, "If X, then what follows or precedes it?"

The SQ3R method is no joke. It's exhaustive and detailed and will take patience and sharp organization to pull off. But if you give yourself the patience and devotion to take each step seriously and slowly, you'll find it incredibly helpful to tackle a complex subject. And each time you do it, it's a little easier than the last.

In explaining the SQ3R method, we briefly skimmed the role of organization and notes and how they impact self-learning. After all, you can't organize everything in your head only and hope to be effective.

Takeaways

- Making the most of your time in the classroom comes down to practicing active and focused listening. Listening is really a collection of many different competencies and happens along five stages.
- During the *reception stage*, we consciously pay attention to new material and make the effort to take it in. In the *understanding stage*, we take what

we've heard and find its meaning and contextualize it, focusing on the purpose of the material and how it's relevant to us.

- In the *evaluating stage*, we consider our own personal evaluation of the material, its quality and application, and whether we agree or like what we've heard. In the *response stage*, we react to the information verbally or nonverbally. Finally, during the *remembering stage*, we revisit what we've heard/learned and recall it with the use of cues to jog our memory.

- In reality, these stages overlap and blur into one another and repeat continually through the learning process. Problems at any stage can mean problems with truly grasping the material overall.

- The HEAR technique can help structure and guide your listening. First, halt (stop what you're doing and focus on what you hear), then engage (by taking notes, asking questions, or paraphrasing), anticipate (predict what will be said next and prepare for it), and replay (review what has been said to cement it in your mind).

- The Peter method of notetaking helps you really digest and *transform* material. There are four stages: normal detailed notetaking, summarizing that information in your own words and noting questions, connecting these ideas to the bigger picture, and summarizing each section to solidify and answer remaining questions. By systematically extracting and rewriting key info, you make your notetaking an active, intelligent process. The SQ3R is a way to process written texts, and consists of five steps: survey, question, read, recite, and review.

- Ultimately, when you can actively ask questions and think critically about the material, you have a better chance of understanding, memorizing, and mastering it.

Chapter 2. Subject Mastery

Teaching Others

You might wonder why a book on learning would include a section on teaching. Rather than teaching and learning being opposites, they are really two aspects of the same single process—in understanding both, we gain a fuller appreciation than if we had examined the subject from just one side or the other.

There is unexpected value in observing how others synthesize information.

First, you will see how someone else learns and absorbs information. Sometimes you can visibly see someone's face light up when they *get it*, and this is no small feat in the process of learning.

Second, you will see how the act of teaching improves the learning of the teacher. In observing how people synthesize information, you can improve upon how *you* do it. Understanding both sides of the coin is a helpful exercise. This, of course, is the process of teaching others to help you yourself learn. This chapter is about how learning to effectively teach others is a great method of learning in itself—and a good skill to have in general.

The Learning Pyramid

Have you ever had the experience of thinking you "know" something, and yet the moment you try to explain that to someone else, it all seems to fall apart? Suddenly, you don't feel so confident in your understanding. Using mind maps and notes are great ways of externalizing info so we can manipulate it clearly, but teaching others is the gold standard in externalization and quickly reveals any gaps or faulty assumptions in our own mental models.

The infamous learning pyramid—also called "the cone of experience"—sheds light on why being able to teach is vital. In fact, much of what we talk about dances around the spectrum of more passive learning as less useful and more active learning as more impactful. This is what the learning pyramid encompasses.

Some may take it as gospel, but the numbers are best if they are seen as rough guidelines. However, they still showcase the different results our learning activities, as learners, retain:

- Ninety percent of what they learn when they teach someone else or use their skills immediately

- Seventy-five percent of what they learn when they practice what they learned

- Fifty percent of what they learn when engaged in a group discussion

- Thirty percent of what they learn when they see a demonstration

- Twenty percent of what they learn from audio-visual

- Ten percent of what they've learned from reading

- Five percent of what they've learned from a lecture

These numbers aren't exact or necessarily even proven. As with most modern theories or modules of education, the learning pyramid faces its share of dissenters. However, it *does* show a general trend that's true: the more involved you are, the better you learn. The more active and deliberate, the better.

Without a doubt, teaching is one of the most involved, participatory, and *non-passive* types of interactions with new information we can have. Like self-explanation and the Feynman technique, teaching someone not only roots information in your mind, it forces you to see what you truly can explain and what you can't. Teaching yourself is good; teaching others is even better.

Teaching exposes the gaps in your knowledge. Having to instruct and explain doesn't let you hide behind generalizations: "Yeah, I know all about how that works. I'll skip it for now." That won't fly if you're explaining a process to someone else—you have to know how every step works and how each step relates to each other. You'll also be forced to answer questions about the information you're teaching, and iron out the exact relationships between ideas.

Having to explain what's going on is essentially a test of your knowledge, and you either know it or you don't. If you can't explain to someone how to replicate something you are teaching, then you actually don't know it yourself. For whatever reason, it's easier to believe you understand something better than you do right up until you're forced to prove it!

Let's take photography as an example. According to the learning pyramid, reading and lecturing combined take up fifteen percent of your retained knowledge, which makes sense: there's only so much you can learn about photography from a textbook or a lectern. Audio-visual aids and seeing demonstrations—what certain angles look like, how to use computers to filter a print—are more helpful in learning to take and process certain pictures. A group discussion about photography would unlock some memorable ideas, and of course, spending the time to practice taking and developing pictures makes solid impressions on your experience.

Now let's examine the bottom (or top, depending on your view) part of the pyramid related to teaching others. You're reinforcing the basic knowledge in others and explaining the principles, types, and general guidelines of photography. Theoretically, you're overseeing all the upper (or lower) segments of the pyramid for students and using your knowledge of the photography process as a guidepost for all of them. And this doesn't even include the pre-instruction time when you're preparing for your own class.

All those teaching activities are active agents that call upon what you already know—and remember when we said you get more from pulling something *out* of your brain than putting stuff *into* it? That's exactly what's happening with that ninety percent tier of the pyramid. You're actively extracting from your previously learned knowledge, sending it out, and reshaping it for others to understand and learn. In turn, that reinforces what you know and deepens your experience in the process.

It's common that you even surprise yourself and find additional insights by explaining and reasoning out loud in a way that simplifies and condenses. Putting vague concepts into concrete words and images can often have a clarifying effect on *your* understanding, not to mention your students'. Teaching forces you to create bite-sized chunks and teach replication—a task you may find far different from explaining theories or concepts.

The Protégé Effect

"Teaching to learn" isn't a radical or even particularly novel concept. In the field of education, it's already regarded as one of the best ways to learn. But there's another element to why teaching can be so helpful to the teacher.

Recent studies have given rise to something researchers call the "protégé effect." This process demonstrates that people who teach others work harder to understand, recall, and apply material more accurately and effectively. There's something about the work required to extend your knowledge and understanding to another mind that makes you more creative, empathetic, and broader minded. Tutors in general therefore score more highly on tests than their non-tutoring counterparts. Why do you think this might be?

To increase the usefulness of this effect, scientists have developed virtual pupils for students to tutor. These virtual students are known as "teachable agents" (TAs). Researchers at Stanford University, which is sort of a hotbed for this kind of technology, explain TAs as follows:

"Students teach their agent by creating a concept map that serves as the agent's 'brain.' An artificial intelligence engine enables the agent to interactively answer questions posed to it by traversing the links and nodes in its map. As the agent reasons, it also animates the path it is following, thereby providing feedback as well as a visible model of thinking for the students. Students can then use the feedback to revise their agent's knowledge (and consequently, their own)."

Students working with a teachable agent are therefore on the opposite side of where they usually are in the typical teaching paradigm—instead of being the student, they're the teacher. The TAs serve as student models, and like all active students, they can ask questions and even give wrong answers. Trials have shown that students using TAs significantly outperform their peers who have only been studying for themselves without TAs to serve as feedback.

Stanford scientists studied the effects of TAs on eighth-grade biology students. Some students were asked to learn biological concepts so they could teach their TAs. The rest were asked to develop an online concept map to demonstrate how their understanding of the concepts was organized. Results showed the students who worked with TAs spent more time engaged with the concept and displayed more motivation to learn. Simply put, the students put forth greater effort to learn for "teaching" their TAs than they did for themselves. They felt responsibility and accountability beyond themselves, and this made them put in the extra work regarding their expertise—the protégés are depending on you!

The scientists at Stanford attributed three factors to the power of the protégé effect:

The ego-protective buffer. This is a sort of psychological shield that allows students to examine failure without the negative feelings it typically produces. This can be a powerful metacognitive force since students are more apt to reflect upon their learning without the emotional sting of disappointment. It's almost like a crash course in cultivating a growth mindset and embracing failure productively.

Incrementalistic view of intelligence. When the learning process is directed externally to support another's learning, students spend more time examining their own understanding. This helps students see how reviewing and revising their insight can impact their own learning.

Sense of responsibility. Teaching another person—or, in this example, the virtual TAs—motivates students to take more command over their own learning process. When they realize that what they say will be absorbed by another thinking unit, they're more meticulous about getting the information right to begin with. Learning is always going to be more effective when we adopt an attitude of conscious and active control over the process, which is something teachers are naturally encouraged to do.

Not all of us who aren't teachers or tutors have the opportunity to share our knowledge directly with willing students. However, thanks again to the miracle of technology, you can find plenty of online sites with message boards or forums all filled with questions you can answer (or at least *find* the answers for).

A nice site to start with—despite its somewhat unruly nature—is Quora.com, where users just literally ask questions of the hive-mind of the internet. Many questions are very general, and some serve as bait for trolls or fanatics. But they're easily funneled out, and you're left with a lot of genuine inquiries asking for serious answers. It's a good, almost comically quick way to share information with others— more importantly, it allows you to reap the rewards of the protégé effect and learn better.

Another way to bring the magic of teaching others into your own study is simply to work in groups with other students and take turns "teaching" one another. And while it's a little corny at first, you can even achieve similar results by *pretending* to teach someone else. Make your own presentation and literally stand up and teach an imaginary person (yes, you can address your pet rock or stuffed toy if it makes it easier!). Ask yourself what questions they might ask, or notice where your explanation seems a little vague or strained.

Examples and Analogy Thinking

If you practice this approach even a little, you'll probably start to notice why it works so well. Do you see how you instinctively reach for examples, metaphors, or little stories to try to bridge the gap between your knowledge and the student's? In order to convey certain concepts, i.e. the *unknown*, it's natural to talk in terms of the *known*. You can consciously draw on the power of analogy, example, and metaphor to enrich your own understanding of the material. This will also help with recall.

Aside from using different types of analogies to improve your retention of learning materials, there are some science-backed tips you can employ to further enhance how productive these analogies can be for your studies. These are:

1) Use multiple analogies for the same topic

This one goes without saying, but using different types of analogies in your learning will ensure that you've grasped your content beyond just a superficial understanding. Since analogies force you to make transfers mentally, they challenge your comprehension of key concepts in different ways depending on the type you use. Generally, it's a good idea to use as many as you can that seem relevant to your topic.

For example, let's say you're learning about the theory of liberalism. The first type of analogy you can use is Antonym. If we think of hot and cold as opposites, what would be a similar antonym for liberalism? This could be either communism or conservatism. Next, we can utilize Example/Type Of analogies. Liberalism is a type of political ideology in the same way that iPhones are a type of smartphone.

A third type of analogy we can attempt is Thing/Characteristic. What is a characteristic of liberalism similar to auditory volume as a characteristic of speakers? One answer is human rights. Likewise, you can utilize multiple analogies for your own concepts and topics.

2) Use examples to constantly reaffirm your learning

This insight has been derived from the studies of Daniel Schwartz and John Bransford. The usage of examples is important because it helps novices and beginners learn through their own knowledge of the content of those examples. Experts can skip examples because they are already intimately aware of the subject matter. But in most instances, examples help you make sense of complex ideas and provide you with tools to remember them more efficiently.

If you're studying ethical systems, make a note of different situations in which they apply. Should you lie to your friend when you don't want to talk to them by saying you're busy? Why or why not? If you have to divide a pie between three people, what would be the fairest way to cut it? Examples like these liven up your studying, as they make dry content much more realistic and relevant to the world around you.

If you can, make your examples as concrete and personally relevant as possible. The more you can tie the abstract concept to "real life," the quicker your student (or you, for that matter) can grasp and contextualize it. Introduce examples and metaphors as part of a dialogue. In the above example, the analogy is introduced by way of a question, which is always more engaging. By leading your student this way, you are guiding them from what they know toward what they don't—clarifying the path for the both of you.

3) Remember the purpose of the analogy

Oftentimes it is easy to use analogies to understand particular concepts mechanically, yet forget why the analogy is appropriate in the first place. For example, if a student is asked what a mitochondria is, they say, "It is the powerhouse of the cell," since that is a standard analogy across biology textbooks. However, many remember the comparison without understanding what it means for mitochondria to be the powerhouse of a cell.

One way to avoid this issue is to frame your analogies in ways that clearly indicate the purpose or role of the comparison. In the case of mitochondria, consider what function it would have to fulfill to be a "powerhouse" for the cell. It would have to provide the cell with power, which is more accurately referred to as energy.

Another thing you can do is list a few drawbacks of the analogy. "Powerhouse" can imply that it merely stores energy, but in fact, mitochondria is responsible for the extracting, processing, and releasing of energy to cells. It isn't enough to simply remember the analogy; you must know why it is an appropriate one to use as well, and these are a few ways to do just that. Remember that any technique you use is only good insofar as it illuminates the material—you're allowed to completely ignore a common analogy if it doesn't actually pull its weight!

4) Reserve analogies for more difficult concepts

While it may be tempting to use analogies throughout your studies, it is advisable to reserve their usage for more complex ideas. Students often find that utilizing analogies for easier concepts and information can cause mental confusion and clutter.

When something is easily understandable, you don't need to break it down further for better retention. You may get yourself in a tangle trying to force a metaphor that doesn't quite fit. Focus your energy on more difficult concepts, especially since you'll be using multiple analogies for the same concept.

Make a list of all the ones you use, list some drawbacks for each, and use visual cues if possible. Employing both visual and text-based cues is a good way to improve retention and understanding according to multimedia learning theory. Also use appropriate comparisons for your analogy on the left-hand side of the academic analogy format. This will make the relation between the main components of your analogy clearer without requiring too much re-reading.

Analogy Thinking

Let's dive a bit deeper into a specific type of analogy thinking.

How might you explain a new business to someone who is clueless in the space? "It's like the Uber of X, except A, B, and C."

When we seek to make ourselves understand an idea, we often default to analogies. They provide instant understanding and context because our thoughts are able to focus on a singular concept and then slowly start to differentiate to the point of comprehension.

And of course, linking new concepts and information through analogy is another great method to cement learning into the knowledge pool. Despite our natural tendencies, analogies are underrated and overlooked as important parts of human cognition. In contrast to this presumption, some neuroscientists, such as Indiana University Professor Douglas Hofstadter, assert that analogies are the foundation of all human thought.

His reasoning is that analogies allow us to understand categories, and categories are how we distinguish information and concepts from each other. It's our ability to identify likenesses—a form of analogy-making—that allows us to discern similarities and thus categorize objects in different ways.

This is easy to see if you consider how we categorize animals. To an untrained eye, a dog and a cat might seem distinctly similar. They both have fur, four legs, and a tail, but their different faces, diets, behavior, and evolutionary heritage allow us to differentiate between the two of them. They are comparable animals, analogous to each other, but they are more closely analogous to their own species, and that is what allows us to place them in their respective categories of dog or cat. But all that means is that we would never use dogs to describe cats, or vice versa.

Even more complex, higher-order ideas are formed by making analogies. Consider the more abstract group of mammal. This group compares dogs to cats while counting them as similar, but also includes animals as diverse as the platypus, dolphin, and opossum. No one would look at a dolphin and believe it was similar to a housecat, but the science is very clear. Lactating, having hair or fur, and being warm-blooded are the criteria that must be met to put creatures into the group of mammal. If they share those characteristics, they are mammals.

Grouping those criteria together allows us to form the higher-order idea of mammal, which enables us to discern which creatures fit the bill. This group of criteria that we simplify into the word *mammal* is what allows us to see dolphins and platypuses as analogous to each other.

Our understanding, and thus the analogies we use to describe the world, evolve as we age and are exposed to ideas in our lives and our cultures. But no matter what we learn, it must be filtered through a brain that categorizes, and thus understands, the world by forming analogies and discerning differences between objects and ideas. When we consciously distinguish different elements and create analogies while learning new information, we speed up the process of integrating our new knowledge into our minds.

Now that we've covered the overall cognitive role and importance of analogy, how can we use it to self-learn and understand more effectively? As we mentioned, analogies provide instant context—a mental model for the information you are looking at—and then you are left to slowly differentiate and flesh out the details.

For instance, earlier we mentioned that new businesses are frequently described as "the Uber of X." Uber is a rideshare company that functions by calling non-taxi drivers to help transport you using their own personal cars. Thus, anything described as "the Uber of X" would be implied to involve people with their own cars, delivering or driving people or things. Okay, we've got a mental image now—a good idea of what's involved, what the purpose is, and how it functions.

Now the important bit of learning comes— how do you differentiate this new business from Uber itself? What nuanced factors make it something other than a clone of Uber? Well, this element, as well as what you are comparing the new business to, is up to you to articulate. When you take a new piece of information and intentionally find a way to create an analogy with it, you are (1) finding a similar model of information that requires understanding enough to compare and contrast two concepts, and (2) further understanding the two models well enough to state how they differ. That's where the deeper learning synthesis occurs.

For instance, what if you wanted to create an analogy around learning the steps involved in creating a new piece of legislation? Abide by the two steps above. You would first find an existing, familiar piece of information that the process for new legislation reminds you of. Search your memory banks for something similar; this type of analysis of major and minor factors is helpful to your learning.

Next, how do they differ? This is where you can clearly demonstrate the difference between concepts, based on a deep understanding. Pick out small details and note how they appear similar but come from totally different motivations. Document what this all means for new legislation.

This is far more than a thought exercise of comparing two different concepts—it's combining old information with new and forcing them to interact toward greater comprehension and memorization.

Bloom's Taxonomy

Another useful tool is called Bloom's taxonomy, created by Benjamin Bloom in 1956 (though updated in 2001) as a way to measure the academic performance of college students. It has since been a staple in academic institutions as a framework for crafting lessons that ensure a thorough comprehension in students. For our purposes, it's a literal step-by-step guideline for what is necessary to move your understanding forward. The magic of this taxonomy comes into play when you **apply** it to your own understanding. When you work with a good teacher, they can identify blocks to your comprehension, identify where you are, and almost prescribe a way forward. They can help you bootstrap your understanding so you can access new material that was once unavailable to you. When you're on your own, it's harder to see what you can't see, never mind see a way past the obstacle. Bloom's taxonomy acts a little like a roadmap for charting your own understanding.

Bloom's taxonomy essentially states that for the highest level of subject understanding (i.e. expertise), there are six sequential levels we must be able to complete. Most people will never make it through all the levels in the taxonomy, so don't let yourself fall victim to that fate. If you are struggling with something, it's possible that you have missed a level beneath the one you're at, or at least that foundation is a bit shaky. The current taxonomy's levels are, from lowest to highest level of understanding, as follows:

- Remember. Retrieving, recognizing, and recalling relevant knowledge from long-term memory.

- **Understand.** Constructing meaning from oral, written, and graphic messages through interpreting, exemplifying, classifying, summarizing, inferring, comparing, and explaining.
- **Apply.** Carrying out or using a procedure for executing or implementing.
- **Analyze.** Breaking material into constituent parts and determining how the parts relate to one another and to an overall structure or purpose through differentiating, organizing, and attributing.
- **Evaluate.** Making judgments based on criteria and standards through checking and critiquing.
- **Create.** Putting elements together to form a coherent or functional whole; reorganizing elements into a new pattern or structure through generating, planning, or producing.

Once you hit the top level of "create," then you can be considered to have a deep grasp on a subject. Yet without advancing through each level of the taxonomy, you can't adequately perform the next levels. We see this illustrated in our lives every day when someone who doesn't have an adequate understanding of a topic seeks to evaluate it and make a judgment upon it. That's because of a failure to follow the taxonomy!

Bloom's taxonomy is a particularly useful tool to help guide and shape your learning process. Basically, the taxonomy is a list of *how* to actively build expertise in a subject matter. It focuses on the mental processes that allow you to frame information and analyze it, each verb a kind of mental tool to grasp and manipulate new incoming data. Bloom's framework is great because it's so versatile and can be used literally anywhere. In the classroom, at work, or in designing your own systems for achieving your personal goals, this taxonomy gives you a shorthand to work with.

The entire taxonomy is predicated on the mental process of learning, which can actually be summed up quite nicely. Before you can **understand** a concept, you must **remember** it. To **apply** a concept, you must first **understand** it. In order to **evaluate** a process, you must have **analyzed** it. To **create** an accurate conclusion, you must have completed a thorough **evaluation**. The challenge is introspection and understanding where you currently fall on the taxonomy, because only then can you pinpoint what is required for you to move forward in your mastery.

Let's dive deeper into each element.

First, *remembering* contains elements like *listening*, *finding* information (using tools like *Googling*, perhaps), actively *memorizing* data, *bookmarking* important information to return to later, *highlighting* key points to synthesize later, and *repeating* information again and again to drill it.

This aspect is all about taking information and fixing it somehow so that you can store it and retrieve it later. If you're the kind of person who likes to make extensive bookmarks and notes about things you want to read or watch in the future, then you are actively remembering. You are also helping your long-term memory put down information whenever you tabulate or place information in easy-to-remember bullet points. Remembering also entails outlining key features or quotes or defining the main ideas so that you can recall the summary later on. Whenever you revise for an exam, you're using these skills.

Understanding happens whenever we engage with information more actively. Whereas remembering is about concretizing and storing information, understanding involves picking it all apart to better see how it works, like some people do to household appliances! *Categorizing* data (like we're doing here), *grouping* information into chunks, *inferring* from the data you have and *predicting* future events based on it, *summarizing*, and *paraphrasing* in different words are all cognitive operations intended to get to the deeper meaning of a set of symbols or patterns.

Teachers who ask their students to write things "in their own words" are doing so because they don't want to test for memorization; they want to test for understanding. If you comprehend a thing deeply, you are able to manipulate it no matter how its components are rearranged or what symbols are used to express it. If you've ever tried to explain something complicated to someone who's not familiar with the concept, you may have found it helpful to give them a related example. You could outline a metaphor from a concept that they'd understand more easily and show how the ideas relate to one another. This *relating* and *associating* is key to developing deep understanding of a topic.

Applying is the third category. This is, broadly, where information is brought into the "real world" and made manifest, whether that's by *executing*, *sketching*, *acting out*, or *articulating*. As you're probably noticing, many of these terms have significant overlap with other verbs in other categories—and this should obviously be the case when you consider that the brain isn't ever truly performing discrete activities, but rather flowing in one continuous action that, for our purposes, we're trying to understand using different models.

In fact, Bloom's verb taxonomy is itself a form of "applying." It's *charting* or

presenting information in a concrete way—
i.e. applying the abstract concepts to make
manifest a model, idea, or concept. *Painting*,
preparing, *displaying*, *reenacting*, and even
playing are all verbs associated with this
category of the taxonomy. Every time you
make a pie chart to illustrate data, turn a
plan into reality, or design an experiment
that actually gets carried out, you're
"applying."

The fourth category is *analyzing*, which is
pretty self-explanatory. Verbs in this
category include *questioning*, *explaining*,
organizing, *deconstructing*, *correlating*, and
calculating. This includes all those verbs
that show us actively operating on and
manipulating information that comes in, not
just to pass it from one form to another, but
to look closely at its constituents, trying to
understand them. Bloom's theory itself is an
example of *appraising* and *categorizing*.
You're participating in these functions
when you draw a mind map, integrate one
set of ideas with another set, break down a
machine into its components, or ask, "Why
is this happening?"

The fifth element is *evaluating*, and it includes any verbs that show we're applying some value judgments to the material in front of us. In the previous category, analysis is value-neutral and merely about understanding. This category, however, concerns things like *criticizing*, *rating*, *reflecting, reviewing*, *assessing*, and *validating*. This is where our brains practice discernment—and the weighing up of the information against stated goals. How useful are the results of your experiment? What is the quality and veracity of the claims you're appraising? How well did you perform? How can you *editorialize* or else compile all this information into a whole that actually says something?

The final verb group is *creating*. Here, our relationship to information is quite fundamental: we make it! *Composing* music, *mixing* known things to create something new, *filming* a movie, *writing* the script, and *role-playing* the characters are all creative ways to engage with information and build something novel. Other creative endeavors you might not have thought of include *programming*, *designing* systems, *adapting* material from one form into another, or even things like *podcasting* or *blogging*. Interestingly, Bloom even considered *leading* to be creative, since leadership often involves guiding people toward an entirely new and self-made vision.

Again, these verbs and categories will always overlap—the point is not to identify discrete categories. Rather, this model is a tool to help you play with information and see it from many different angles in the same way as a toolbox of differently colored glasses could be worn to look at the same information in varying lights. When you're trying to learn and memorize, it makes a huge difference to engage actively and deliberately with information—not just in one or two ways, but in as many as possible. This way, data comes alive, becoming three-dimensional and allowing you a depth of understanding that will last longer than more shallow impressions.

Whenever you're learning something new, you might, for example, highlight the text in the book so you can summarize it (remembering) and then paraphrase that text in your own words (understanding). You can then apply your understanding by constructing your own chart or diagram (applying) and taking some time to break that diagram down, question it, and link it to other diagrams you've already made (analyzing). You can ask yourself after all this whether these methods are actually helping you retain the material (evaluating) and use your assessment to guide the further development of improved systems of learning (creating).

It sounds tedious, and it can be, but that's the true path to information synthesis. In fact, it's this tough mental work and struggle that really cements concepts and facts in your brain.

Learning from Mistakes

We will look a little closer at learning from failures and mistakes in a later chapter, but it's worth mentioning here as well. In most situations, we tie accomplishment with success: winning, positive outcomes, and finding solutions. After all, isn't that the whole point of trying to improve our study strategy? But the irony is that in learning, a key component in achievement is *failing*. And that is something that few of us are taught to do properly. Consequently, we don't value failure as much as we should, and we miss out on the lessons it has for us.

Productive failure is an idea identified by Manu Kapur, a researcher at the National Institute of Education in Singapore. The philosophy builds on the learning paradox, wherein *not* arriving at the desired effect is as valuable as prevailing, if not more. You might already agree that learning to manage disappointment, cultivate a resilient attitude, and persist through difficulty are important for learning. But productive failure is not about the emotional impact, but rather, the neurological impact. In other words, it's worth learning to master failure not just because of its psychological benefits, but because it can concretely improve your cognitive prowess.

Kapur stated that the accepted model of instilling knowledge—giving students structure and guidance early and continuing support until the students can get it on their own—might not be the best way to actually promote learning. Although that model intuitively makes sense, according to Kapur, it's best to let students flounder by themselves without outside help.

Kapur conducted a trial with two groups of students. In one group, students were given a set of problems with full instructional support from teachers onsite. The second group was given the same problems but received no teacher help whatsoever. Instead, the second group of students had to collaborate to find the solutions.

The supported group was able to solve the problems correctly, while the group left to itself was not. But without instructional support, this second group was forced to do deeper dives into the problems by working together. They generated ideas about the nature of the problems and speculated on what potential solutions might look like. They tried to understand the root of the problems and what methods were available to solve them. Multiple solutions, approaches, and angles were investigated that ended up providing a three-dimensional understanding of the problems.

The two groups were then tested on what they had just learned, and the results weren't even close. The group without teacher assistance *significantly outperformed* the other group. The group that did not solve the problems discovered what Kapur deemed a "hidden efficacy" in failure: they nurtured a deeper understanding of the structure of the problems through group investigation and process.

The second group may not have solved the problem itself, but they learned more about the aspects of the problem. Going forward, when those students encountered a new problem on another test, they were able to use the knowledge they generated through their trial more effectively than the passive recipients of an instructor's expertise.

Consequently, Kapur asserted that the important parts of the second group's process were their miscues, mistakes, and fumbling. When that group made the active effort to learn by themselves, they retained more knowledge needed for future problems. At the time, these students probably felt unsure of themselves, and it might have been unpleasant to grapple with something they were so unsure about. But in truth, this discomfort was not a sign that anything was going wrong—in fact, they were in the middle of a powerful learning experience.

Three conditions, Kapur said, make productive failure an effective process:

- Choose problems that "challenge but do not frustrate."

- Give learners the chance to explain and elaborate their processes.

- Allow learners to compare and contrast good and bad solutions.

Struggling with something is a positive condition to learning, though it requires discipline and a sense of delayed gratification. This runs counter to our instincts. How can we, so to speak, let failing work for us?

Chances are you'll come across a moment or two of defeat in your process, along with the temptation to give up. You may even sense this before you start, which can lead to crippling anxiety that can hover over your work.

Expect but don't succumb to frustration.

Anticipating frustration in advance is just good planning—but you also have to plan for how to deal with it. Sketch out a plan or idea on how to alleviate frustration when it happens—most often, this will be taking a break from the situation to recharge and getting some momentary distance from the problem. Quite often, the mere act of pausing allows for objectivity to seep in, letting you see the hang-up more clearly. But in any case, it will abate the most immediate anxieties you're feeling and give you the chance to approach the issue from a more relaxed frame of mind.

It's a matter of being comfortable with a state of mental discomfort and confusion. This can be akin to juggling ten balls in the air at once and not being sure when you can place them down.

Learning mode is different from results mode, and they have entirely different measures of success. When you want to learn, you are just looking for an increase in knowledge—*any* increase is successful learning. Reframe your expectations to make the learning as important as the result—*more* important, if possible.

Explicit and static knowledge, such as facts and dates, doesn't necessarily benefit from this. It doesn't need to. But transmitting deep and layered comprehension cannot just be plugged into the brain. It must be manipulated and applied, and failure is inherent in that process. In a way, failures function similarly to the types of questions we discussed in an earlier chapter, where they slowly allow you to triangulate knowledge and understanding based on what's *not* working and what's *not* true.

In the end, failure acts as a blueprint for our next steps. It is a test run that didn't go as planned and thus allows you to rectify pinpointed matters for the future.

For example, let's say you're planting a vegetable garden, noting the steps and techniques you use along the way, and when it's time to harvest, some of your plants don't come out the way they are supposed to. Is it because you used the wrong soil? Use your resources to find out *why* that soil was wrong and what it needs to look like. Was the failed plant too close to another? Learn techniques for maximizing placement within a small space.

Hidden in all of this is the fact that living and acting to avoid failure, even just in learning, leads to very different results than someone who actively seeks success. One approach wants to limit exposure and risk, while the other is focused on the end goal no matter the cost. Failure doesn't have to be your friend, but it *will* be your occasional companion, like it or not. With that in mind, it probably makes more sense to embody the approach that is about taking more risk—and also reaping greater rewards.

Takeaways

- By learning to teach others, we deepen our own understanding and retention, since we uncover a richer and more fundamental appreciation of the concepts behind the material. Compared to other strategies, teaching others may have the highest chance of improving recall and comprehension.

- The protégé effect is the observation that students who teach others do better, perhaps because they learn incrementally, take responsibility for the learning process, and are "ego-protected" from the prospect of failure.

- Analogies, examples, and metaphors are powerful tools to convey new concepts. To use them effectively in teaching/learning, make use of as many different analogies as possible and mix them in frequently, using examples to illustrate. Only use those analogies that actually work (i.e. don't forget their purpose) and reserve them more complex topics, since they may only confuse simpler ideas.

- Bloom's taxonomy is a roadmap to chart one's understanding and mastery of a topic. It can be used to identify the next step we need to take to deepen our grasp. Each step depends on mastery of the steps before it, although it's not necessary to achieve all stages.

- The stages are: remember, understand, apply, analyze, evaluate, and create. If you're struggling with the material, you can diagnose your position in the taxonomy and then attempt to overcome the obstacle by engaging with tasks from the next level. You can also avoid working at one level when you haven't achieved the previous ones—and confusing yourself further.

- Productive failure is the name given to mistakes, fumbling, or errors that actually illuminate our understanding better than simply being told the correct approach. Figuring things out for yourself can feel difficult in the moment, but it gives you a richer and more nuanced grasp of the material. The lesson is to embrace the learning curve, including mess ups and uncertainty, and use failure to drive understanding.

Chapter 3. Making a Plan and Managing Your Time

Your Perfect Study Environment

Let's get organized. Now, before we begin, I know—a lot of this is not exactly going to look like rocket science. The thing is, though, something can be simple without being easy. So many of us just dive right into our studies without a second thought because we (wrongly) assume that the best practice is so obvious that we'll do everything right without trying. Admit it— you've sat down with a textbook and highlighter, ready to "study" without a very clear idea of what that actually means!

First things first: the right location. If you have access to a school or university library, or a quiet room with a desk at home or at work, then that's a great place to start. Not all of us have a lot of choices when it comes to where we study, but we can always work with what we have. You may have a split schedule that means you study in several places throughout the day. Depending on your own unique cognitive preferences and thresholds for stimulus, you may work best in a deadly silent room with zero distractions, or you may benefit from the so-called "coffee shop effect" where you get in the zone when surrounded by gentle white noise around you.

Where to Study

Spare a moment to actually consider how your study needs are currently being met by the available options in your life. The following are certainly good to have, but you may prioritize them differently or simply not care about certain criteria:

- a good source of light so you can read and write without strain—natural light in the day and an adjustable lamp at night are great

- a computer or device if you need one, with appropriate software
- all your study materials in one place, properly organized and within reach
- a desk and proper chair, adjusted properly to give ergonomic support
- quiet and distraction free (as much as is possible)
- comfortable—you'll be spending lots of time here, so it makes sense to create a space you genuinely feel able to relax in and immerse yourself in your work

You may need to invest in some storage or a better quality desk lamp, or you may need to completely rethink your study setup. The perfect environment is like a stage set for learning—the fewer distractions, the better. Being organized is not just a question of staying tidy (although this matters too!) but rather about managing the external environment so you can support the internal environment. Organized on the outside means clear, clean, and focused on the inside.

Before you rush out to splurge on dozens of binders and folders, bear in mind that the simplest filing system is usually the best. Your notes, books, and journals need to be organized the way your own brain is organized—i.e. logically indexed and arranged so that you can easily retrieve what you need when you need it. You don't need to reinvent the wheel, though. Use simple color-coding or old-school techniques like big-ring binders that you can manage under separate sections as needed. Try to have a single portable journal or notebook that coordinates everything so you can see at a glance what you're doing each day. This is especially important if you're moving around a lot or studying on the fly and need to pack a bag with that day's assignments. You may also like to use apps or software to manage articles and papers digitally, depending on your course material. Evernote is a popular one, but there are almost thousands to choose from to suit your needs.

When to Study

When you hear "study environment," you may immediately think of an ideal place, but the time of day or week you choose to study also forms an important part of the background atmosphere of your study efforts. Just as you want to maximize the space you have, you need to maximize not only your time but your energy levels over time. Ask yourself the following questions to zoom in on the ideal study schedule for you:

- What times of day am I naturally most energized, motivated, and focused? How can I align my study periods with these bouts of energy?
- How have I scheduled my other obligations, and what time does that leave me for studying? Can I move things around?
- How many hours per week do I need to study? Is this realistic, and if not, what needs to change?
- Do I have enough room in my schedule for sleep, relaxation, and living my life?
- What happens if I miss a study session—how flexible is my schedule,

and can I make it up some other time?

- How long can I concentrate at a maximum? Does my schedule reflect my natural cognitive limits?
- What am I doing to remove distractions and interruptions, i.e. how am I maintaining and defending this schedule? Is it working?

It's easy to have grand, impressive-sounding ideas when putting together a study plan. Maybe you don't quite grasp how unrealistic it is to schedule a three-hour non-stop study session after dinner, on a weeknight, when the rest of the family is watching a movie. Sadly, this can lead to you writing yourself off as lazy or having a procrastination problem when, inevitably, the grand plan falls flat and Netflix wins yet again. Sure, it's a question of discipline and willpower . . . but with a smart, realistic plan made well ahead of time, you won't *need* so much discipline and willpower to get things done!

Studying is Not an Event; It's a Habit

No personal trainer in the world will tell you that a single great workout is enough to get fit and stay fit, and no nutritionist will call your diet healthy just because you had one really impressive salad one Tuesday afternoon. In the same way, becoming good at studying is not about any single behavior or achievement. It's about consistent repeated actions and their cumulative effect. In other words, a habit.

Any behavior change will be hard at first, and then easier once it becomes automatic and routine. Getting started is the hardest part. The second hardest part is *not stopping*. Making efficient and intelligent learning skills a part of your normal everyday life means incorporating good habits. Daily. Until doing the right thing is actually easier and more automatic than doing the wrong thing.

The first habit to master is **scheduling**.

Scheduling is a commitment you make to yourself. You set your intention, write it down in words, and tell your brain, "This is happening." Importantly, don't just think about what you'll do—write it down. Things that are in black and white are psychologically more fixed and real.

Time is a precious resource and needs to be consciously budgeted. If you don't deliberately block out periods of study time on your calendar, life has a funny way of filling it up for you. You have to consistently cordon off areas of your life that are *only for study*. And that's non-negotiable. Never mind for now what you're missing during these periods, first just make the commitment that this time is dedicated to study.

There are many different scheduling techniques and approaches out there, but as with most things, simple is usually best. If you want to fit ten hours of study into your week, spread them out evenly, making sure to give yourself a day or two rest. Break the study periods up rather than have a single long session, and make sure you're scheduling in enough time to settle in, orient, and recap at the end.

Studying at regular intervals is a good habit, but learning to schedule is in itself also a good habit. At the end of every week, schedule time where you sit down and appraise last week's schedule (What didn't work? Why? How can you do better next week?) and draw up next week's schedule. Don't become complacent—continually reassess your plans and tweak as you go along.

The second good habit is to **make a list**.

So, you've blocked in the time, now you need to decide what you're doing with it. A checklist shapes and structures your time, giving it focus so that you are using the period as efficiently as possible. Here's an example of a checklist you can follow for every study period:

1. Make sure the desk is cleared and all the materials are ready
2. Turn off phone and set the internet browser blocker on for the next hour (to stop you from getting distracted online)

3. Get a glass of water or tea and maybe a snack
4. Make sure your area is comfy, well lit, and quiet, and no distractions are waiting in the wings to derail you
5. Set a timer to buzz at the end of the period.

You can include a short meditation or stretching session at the start or end. You can begin each session with a few minutes to review what you did last time, and end it with a recapping exercise like making a summary, mind map, list of what you've learned, or set of questions to tackle in the next session.

The third habit is to **contain your worries.**

Worrying about not doing well or failing an exam is a distraction. These anxieties can run away with you if they're not contained and minimized. New research is suggesting that writing down your fears and concerns can help alleviate them. Keep a small "worry journal" and note down the things that are bugging you. See this offloading as a way to temporarily set down concerns so you can study unhindered.

You could do a visualization or ritual to symbolize that you're setting these aside for the time being. You can always come back to them later. If anxiety is a significant problem for you, one of the best things you can do for your grades is to work with a counselor to help you manage these feelings so they don't interfere with your work.

Finally, an essential habit is to **plan your study**.

This is your roadmap through the study session itself. No, it's not enough to sit down and bumble your way through the material—you need to know what you're doing, for how long, and why. Jot down some notes at the beginning of every session to keep you focused:

- What material exactly are you covering today?
- What things are you *not* covering today?

- What are you actually doing with this material? (think in terms of verbs: summarizing, analyzing, solving, scanning, etc.)
- How does this plan fit into the overall outline for the week? How does it contribute to your overall objectives?

You don't need to spend long doing this—with practice, it will literally take a minute or so. The results, however, will save you enormous amounts of time and energy.

Make a Study Plan

Let's take a closer look at planning. As they say, if you fail to plan, you plan to fail, and this is sadly all too true when it comes to studying. Planning in detail isn't a punishment—it's there to make your life easier. If you plan well, you avoid (stressful!) last minute cramming and actually retain more. There are a few golden rules when planning out your study week:

Always be prepared
Review everything you cover
Mix it up

Start early

Let's begin with **preparation**. Remember active listening? Well, you need to be active here, too. Before you even begin, prepare by asking yourself what you know and what you don't know. Like using a map, you can only chart a course if you know where you're aiming for and where you're starting from. A good rule of thumb is to always try to generate your own materials—don't simply read through texts. Create your *own* summaries, mind maps, tests, flashcards, outlines, and quizzes. These perform double duty—you learn when you make them, and you learn again when you use them.

The way you identify and organize the material into a logical structure is up to you and depends on your topic. But you could try making summary pages, outlines, concept maps, charts, diagrams, lists, flow charts, or a collection of problems or questions you're curious about. A word of warning: your goal in producing these things is not for the sake of producing them. It's not about creating *beautiful-looking* notes—it's about supporting your own internal organization and understanding. Be on the lookout; if a strategy interferes with the material rather than simplifying or illuminating it, just ditch it.

"Preparation" might be the wrong word since what you're doing is the actual bulk of your learning. Make a list of concepts and move from basic to more complex, simple to more detailed. Lay the groundwork with the big ideas and then fill in as you go. Yes, it sounds basic, but the reason you're being so deliberate is because most people actually overestimate their understanding until they're forced to lay it all out step by step. Rather than find out that you only have a superficial understanding on the day you write your exam, unearth your misconceptions early on and dig into them.

Reviewing is on the other side of this coin. It's also active, however. Rather than seeing what you don't know (and hence what you still need to grasp), you are asking yourself what you've learned, and how much ground you've covered. You become your own teacher. Again, the goal is not to win prizes or feel bad about not getting something right, but to see where you are with your learning so that you can adjust and carry on.

During learning you *absorb*. During the review process, you *release*. Try explaining in different ways what you've learned to others. (This is way, way more effective than you'd think.) Complete a quiz or mock test and grade yourself—but look beyond the grade and ask what you didn't get right, why, and how you can tackle these topics better next time. Work through problems or flashcards, or simply try to recall as much of a process or sequence as you can from memory. Write an essay or reproduce an important diagram. You can do any of the above with a friend, where you mutually quiz and grade one another simultaneously.

As you can see, preparation and reviewing can be done on a repeating loop. You ask, "What don't I know?" and your answer concerns a particular process in chapter five. You plan to tackle it in a study session. At the end of the session, you do a few quizzes and test yourself—can you recite the process? How do you perform on a mini-quiz on this topic? In a way, reviewing is actually preparation for the next step of the study process. You may see that you understand more than before, but still need to work on a particular section. You plan it for next time and repeat, fine tuning your understanding.

Cramming doesn't work. What does work is "little as often." Spread work out as much as possible and use both preparation and review to anchor each block. Give yourself time and space between each new concept for the material to sink in. Drill the content in by constantly asking where you are, what you've learned, what is still tricky. This keeps you on track and stops you from wasting time. Small incremental steps achieve bigger results than trying to do everything all at once. This is the reasoning behind the rule to **switch things up**. Do a little prep, a little work, then review. Repeat at varying intervals. Use your review to guide the next task. When you review, do it in different ways each time. Finally, **starting early** is what allows you to take your time to get all this reviewing and preparation done. Think of your study material like a big meal—you want to digest it slowly bit by bit with enough time to thoroughly chew and digest each bite!

You've broken your calendar down into time chunks, and now you can break the material down into conceptual chunks. It sounds a little too basic, but it really comes down to breaking things into smaller manageable pieces and tackling just one or two pieces at a time, making sure that each one is thoroughly grasped and understood before going on to the next. It doesn't matter if you break things down by chapter, theme, lecture, or chronological order. Just make sure that for every block of time you have scheduled on your calendar, you are building in both preparation and review of a small relevant chunk.

How much time for each? That depends. Aim at first for two hours to prepare and thirty minutes to review. But if your subject is more hands-on or you're struggling with it, increase the review time.

For non-technical topics like English, history, or psychology, your organization is going to largely be *conceptual*. You need to know what the big themes, topics, trends, arguments, and ideas are, and how to explain them, compare them, and evaluate them. For this, consider constructing mind maps or concept maps where you outline the broad themes and then nest the smaller ideas within that. Make sure you're familiar with definitions and have engaged fully with the material by valuating it, arguing for or against it, and analyzing it through many different lenses. This is especially true if you need to generate unique responses. Try practice essays or go over past exam papers to familiarize yourself with the question format.

For more technical topics, your focus is likely to be more *procedural*. Work through problems and learn the steps so you can extrapolate to other worked problems. Do practice tests and quizzes. Draw charts, flow charts, and diagrams that help you encapsulate ideas into one place. Focus on *how* to solve the various problems by seeing where you go wrong on test questions.

But again, don't get too wedded to any one particular method or approach—just remember that the technique is there to serve you. If it's not helping, try something else. Keep experimenting until you find something that fits your work style, your topic, and your level of understanding. You may discover that the best approach is to use a variety of different techniques as needed.

A Lifestyle that Supports Learning

So, we've looked at how to block off study periods and what to do during those times. To recap (i.e. what we've been recommending all throughout the last section!):

1. Decide where you will study and create an optimal environment
2. Decide when you'll study and schedule blocks of time
3. Devise a study routine you always follow
4. Make a study plan every week for what you'll cover in each block

5. Include periods of **preparation** and periods of **review**, alternating
6. Start early, build good habits, and regularly appraise and adjust as you go

Now, let's consider all those things *outside* of your study window period. It's obvious when you think about it, but what you do when you're not studying also has a significant impact on how well you do when you are. For example, if you were up all night partying and are completely hungover the next day, it doesn't matter how well you've prepped or what plans you've made for yourself. You're simply not going to get much done!

As a student, all your focus naturally goes on your cognitive abilities. It's all about your ability to think, how much you remember, your intelligence, your dedication and habits, and so on. No matter how abstract this all is, however, it eventually comes down to your *physical* brain, which is as much a part of your body as your arms or legs. If you are physically overtired, unhealthy, stressed, or ill, there's no amount of willpower or good intention that will save you.

So, it's about creating good study routines and skills, but also good life habits in general so they can support us as we do the very best we can with our studies. All the advice below is going to sound completely obvious, but all you have to do is notice how seldom people *actually follow* this advice to know that getting it right is not as easy as it looks.

What is a "healthy lifestyle," anyway?

It goes beyond preventing disease or avoiding things that are bad for us. It's also about proactively supporting our *complete* wellbeing, which means our physical health, our social life and relationships, our hobbies, our work/life balance, our sleep, our exercise routines, and even our greater sense of purpose and connection in life. A hangover is a pretty big obstacle to studying, but it's actually not as bad as chronic untreated depression, for example, or a diet that consistently leaves you feeling tired and lethargic.

Rest is Non-negotiable

It's a mistake to think of rest as the opposite of work. When you rest, you are recuperating, digesting, and consolidating—you are not merely wasting time. Rest is not doing nothing. It's a necessary part of life—when we expend energy, our bodies need a period afterward to recover. Always. In the gym, if you constantly push yourself and never rest, the result is usually an injury or illness, not to mention sub-par performance. It's the same with studying. Forcing yourself through a study session when you're overtired doesn't make you a dedicated genius. It just means you do a poor job and waste time, probably feeling awful in the process.

Quality rest means time for your brain to just be still. Turn off devices and glowing pixelated screens and unwind. Take long walks to stretch your muscles, meditate, stretch, have a long bath, or enjoy a sociable meal with friends. Zoning out in front of the TV when you should be sleeping is *not* quality rest, nor is wasting hours of time gaming or browsing junk on the internet.

Practice good "sleep hygiene," too, by going to bed and waking up each day at the same time. Make sure you have a dark, comfortable, quiet room, a good mattress, and breathable bed clothes, and ban devices from your bedroom and from the thirty minutes prior to sleep.

Eat to Support Your Brain

It's not really possible for a person to drastically change their IQ. But your cognitive performance *can* be impacted by a number of things, one of the biggest being your overall nutrition. It's hard to focus if you're hungry, overfull, or living on a diet of junk food, alcohol, and caffeine. And it's no exaggeration to say that a vitamin deficiency or chronic dehydration could make the difference between scraping through a test and getting a solid B+.

Don't take your brain for granted! It works hard for you, and with only a small amount of care and respect, it will continue to work hard for you.

- Avoid extremes—fasting and bingeing can wreak havoc on your blood sugar, which interferes with your energy levels but also with your motivation. Similarly, avoid huge doses of sugar, which can leave you groggy and lethargic afterward (not to mention looking for the next hit)
- Make each meal a good balance of unrefined carbohydrates, good fat, and protein. Low carb diets are notorious for undermining cognitive performance—your brain prefers to run on glucose!
- As usual, get as many fruits and vegetables in your diet as possible
- Keep hydrated
- Caffeine can enhance cognitive performance and focus, but only up to a point. Know your limits and avoid caffeine after lunch
- It goes without saying, but moderate alcohol. Too much impacts your immune system, dampens motivation, and can impair memory.

You may also find that drinking makes it easier to procrastinate or flake on your study commitments

- Take a multivitamin that includes B vitamins and vitamin D, deficiencies of which can both seriously hinder your focus and concentration. Certain performance enhancing supplements (like ginseng or ashwagandha) *may* be useful, but you don't strictly need them

Stress Management is Your Responsibility

Your emotional and mental state of mind are a fundamental part of your health. Chronic stress, anxiety, or depression are perhaps the *biggest* obstacles to efficient learning. It's not always our fault if we are dealing with family or relationship issues, have money worries, or are experiencing difficult feelings about our studies in general. But it *is* our responsibility to do what we can to support our own mental health and wellbeing.

This means being honest about when we are struggling, and asking for help when necessary. It means having the courage to practice self-care and take action when we realize that our mental health is not what it could be and is getting in the way of us reaching our full potential.

This is not to say that you should wait until you have a full-blown personal crisis before you act—in fact, the opposite. Good mental health also means regularly releasing stress built up each day and working through small problems as they arise so they don't become big problems. If you're reading this book, there's a strong chance you already understand the value of taking conscious responsibility for your future and doing what you can to improve on your blind spots and weaknesses.

Is there a relationship, bad habit, family dynamic, history of trauma, or problem with low self-esteem that is getting between you and your study goals? Do you need to work on better boundaries? Then the onus is on you to seek out the resources that will empower you to overcome the issue.

Scientifically Proven Methods for Studying

Declutter

The Princeton Neuroscience Institute has found evidence for the fact that a tidy desk means a tidy mind. Psychology researcher Sabine Kastner finds that, contrary to much-loved "nutty professor" stereotypes about thriving in cluttered spaces, the brain actually performs better when only the materials currently needed are at hand.

It comes down to distraction. By taking fMRIs of subjects performing a simple scanning task, they noticed that neural activity was dominated not by what the brain could see, but by what it was looking for. It takes effort to mentally supress irrelevant details in the environment; by reducing clutter and distraction, you free your brain up to focus more, rather than constantly giving it the work of filtering out unnecessary stimuli. The takeaway? Keep only what you need for the current task on your desk. Clear everything else away.

Take a Deep Breath

A study done at the Trinity College Institute of Neuroscience finds that deep breathing can alter the body's production of the neurotransmitter noradrenaline. Regulated noradrenaline levels mean you feel calmer and more focused. It's not rocket science: before you start studying, pause, close your eyes, and take a slow, deep belly breath through your nose for a count of four seconds. Hold it for two seconds, then slowly let it go. Repeat a few times and notice how different you feel.

Get Out of Bed

If you study in the same place as you sleep, it's obvious you're going to make some unhealthy associations that will interfere with both your ability to sleep and to study! The Division of Sleep Medicine at Harvard University recommends having a designated study place that's not your bed—but you already knew that!

Keep an Even Temperature

A 2006 study by Seppanen et. al. at Cornell University found that the optimal range for study and work is around twenty-two to twenty-five degrees Celsius. Keep an eye on your overall temperature and adjust accordingly.

Takeaways

- Effective studying is all about carefully managing your time and resources. It's also about making sure you set the stage for success and create an environment conducive to learning. Set up a comfortable, quiet, and distraction-free zone where you study.
- Decide what time of the day and week you'll study according to your own rhythms and preferences. Shorter, more frequent sessions are ideal, planned regularly when you're most energetic and able to focus. Block out this time on a weekly schedule.
- Studying well is more of a long-term habit than an isolated event. Commit to designing a strategy that works for you.

First, make a list that you follow every session to keep momentum.

- Make sure you're doing something to manage and contain stress and anxiety, such as meditation, journaling, or scheduling time to tackle fears and concerns without them jeopardizing your work.

- When you make your study plan, focus on two alternating components: preparation and review. In preparation, you generate unique and personal notes, summarize, organize concepts, and work through new ideas. In review, you consolidate what you've covered by testing yourself or doing worked examples. How much time you spend on each will depend on your topic and your level of mastery.

- Make sure you are regularly alternating these two aspects and mixing up both your prep and review portions with diversified approaches. The sooner you start, the sooner you can see what works and what doesn't and adjust accordingly.

- A lifestyle that supports learning is a healthy lifestyle; sleep enough, eat well, and consciously manage stress levels.

Make sure you have regular rest periods to bank what you learn.

- There are some scientifically proven techniques for getting the most from your study sessions, including deep breathing, decluttering your workspace, keeping an optimal temperature, and making sure you never study in your bed.

Chapter 4. Memory Techniques

So you've made yourself organized, created a realistic study plan, and gotten your mindset clear by making your workspace clear. The stage is set. Let the studying begin!

In this chapter, we dive right into the cognitive skill you're probably thinking of most when you imagine yourself preparing for an important exam: memory. The bad news is that few of us are naturally gifted with the ability to effortlessly remember everything without trying. But the good news is that almost everyone can learn to make the best of their brain's natural competencies and improve their memory—without cramming. The key is to understand how your brain naturally likes to process and store information, and then work *with* rather than *against* these preferences.

Technique 1: Use Images

A picture really is worth a thousand words. Studies done at the MIS Research Center at the University of Minnesota finds that we process visual data *sixty thousand times faster* than words, and that ninety percent of the data we process is visual. It's clear: our brain speaks in the language of pictures. You can use this fact to your advantage by deliberately converting information into visual data that is much easier to perceive, process, store, and retrieve (i.e. to learn!).

Let's say you want to memorize a complicated series of political events for a history exam. The written dates and their corresponding events are tough to remember. Instead, you could lay the info visually: draw a cartoon with the crucial events (the funnier and more bizarre, the better) and put them in chronological sequence. It's far easier to remember which thing came first when you can visually recall their position on the page in your mind's eye.

The idea is to take bits of data and convert them into a form that feels relatively effortless to remember. Close your eyes right now and see how difficult it is to remember the position of different items in your room or on your desk. Chances are, you can *easily* recall this data even without much rote memorization. So, the next time you have to remember, say, a sequence of ten items, try this: assign each item to an object in your room or home and make an obvious connection between them.

For example, if you need to remember the steps in the photosynthetic chain, assign each process to a room in your house and chart a walk-through so you remember the details in order. The light reaction takes place in your sunroom, whilst the Calvin/dark reaction happens in your bedroom, which is darker. Picture the granum in the chloroplast as your bookshelf, the different items on your bedside table as different molecules or reactions, and so on.

It doesn't need to be as complicated as this, however. Just make sure that you're taking verbal information (which is relatively expensive, cognitively speaking) and converting it into pictures, ideas, diagrams, colors, or concrete objects in your real world. This is, after all, the form of data your brain evolved to manage best.

The more meaningful, outrageous, or funny the images, the better they'll stick. Make rude anagrams to help you remember lists, and conjure up specific images in your mind as you do. To remember the directions on a compass, you can remember "never eat silkworms" for north, south, east, and west in a clockwise direction. You can enrich this, though, by visually imagining that little worm on the world map, chewing a hole in the Big Apple in New York, to the west. If you always spell "pronunciation" wrong, imagine a stern, angry *nun* who is reminding you of that crucial error you make in the middle. If you're learning to write Arabic and can't remember how letters connect, give each a visual personality and imagine each letter's "hands" and who they want to be friends with, and who they don't. You get the picture (pun very much intended!).

Technique 2: Create Mnemonics and Acronyms

It's easier to remember one word than it is to remember five. So, if you can turn five words into one, you've actually multiplied your memory by a factor of five. The classic example is BODMAS, to help you remember which mathematical operation to perform in which order—B is for brackets, O is for orders and powers, D is for division, and so on. You just have to remember one bit of information (the word "bodmas") and not six, plus their order.

A mnemonic is a little phrase or sentence that helps you remember a rule or principle. For example:

- It's spelled grAy in America and grEy in England.

- ROYGBIV can help you remember the colors of the rainbow in order. Maybe you can picture a flamboyant rainbow colored mascot called Roy G. Biv.
- Mnemonics can be physical too—using your knuckles to remember the number of days in each month or using your fingers in the "right hand rule" in physics to remember, for example, the orientation of thrust, field of motion, and current.
- Speaking of which, if you can't remember the difference between "current" and currant," you can remember that the "ant" in currant is a little ant stealing crumbs from a currant bun.
- Rhymes and alliteration can help—if you're working DIY at home, remember "righty tighty, lefty loosey."
- To quickly remember the letters of notes in music, remember "every good boy does fine" for the notes E, G, B, D, F.
- To remember the difference between "their" and "there," literally picture

the "I" in the former as a little man, while the "r" in the latter is a sign board pointing over "there."

Now, don't create acronyms and rhymes and so on just for the sake of it. You may find that it's actually quite hard to recall strange and nonsensical sentences out of the blue—and if you do forget them, you forget everything else and will be completely stranded. Instead, try to make your mnemonics and acronyms as powerful as possible by making them relevant to your brain. Make them unique to you (include things and people from your own life), make them emotive (for example, build in strong emotions like love or anger, or add in swear words or comedic elements you'll never forget), and use vivid imagery that makes meaningful sense to you.

It's a good idea to think about giving your mnemonic a "handle." This is something that will help you retrieve those memories when you need them, a bit like a tag or file name that helps you find it in a pile of stored memories. Let's say you want to remember the value for pi. You could remember the phrase "May I have a pillow?"—the number of letters in each word tells you the figures in order, i.e. 3.1416. The "handle" is that pillow begins with the letters **pi**. This makes it a more powerful mnemonic than a weird sentence like "for I know a sailor" because there is no handle to connect it to the concept of pi. It's likely more difficult to remember this strange sentence fragment than it is to simply remember five digits!

While you're at it, make sure you can actually visualize what pi is—it's the circumference divided by the diameter. If you can actually picture the diameter of a circle being fitted into the circumference, you can guess that it's roughly three times with a bit extra to spare. That means if you get a figure for pi that is closer to 3.6, then you know something has gone wrong.

Technique 3: Tell Stories

You've probably already noticed that there's a lot of overlap between the technique of visual imagery and mnemonics—and that's good! If you create a verbal mnemonic that has visual and physical elements, rhyming, humor, personal significance, and data that speaks to all five senses, you are essentially giving any piece of information a rich, three-dimensional representation in your brain, making it far easier to remember.

Your brain was built to navigate a visual world and to make meaning of disparate elements by bringing them into one coherent, intelligible whole. In other words, our brains are built for storytelling and not for dispassionately processing isolated, unconnected bits of information. Make life easier for yourself by turning anything you want to memorize into a narrative. You may have seen that we already did a little of this in the examples for the previous two techniques—it seems that the brain can't help but make up stories, even without your conscious effort!

Let's say you're studying chemistry and trying to memorize some important equations and facts. You can picture each element on the left side of the equation as a person at a party, and then on the right side as after the party is over. There's a bit of scandal—the carbon, hydrogen, and oxygen combined to form a love triangle (in the end, it was sweet, literally—they formed glucose and left together), the water got hot tempered and left early as vapor, and the poor catalyst who introduced everyone was left just the same after as before, unchanged, although he paid for all the drinks and invited everyone.

The key here is to tell stories that you actually *want* to remember. You have no trouble remembering juicy secrets, hilarious events, or scary horror stories, right? Build in emotion, human drama, connection, shocking surprises, and so on. Your brain has a preference for this kind of material.

Maybe you're trying to remember the different anatomical structures of the brain. You remember that the region at the very back of the brain is the cerebellum by thinking of your friend, Sarah Billingham. She has a low ponytail at the back of her head (that's how you remember the location of this brain region) and she works as a kindergarten teacher.

You tell yourself a story about the three things she does every day. She wakes up and goes to the gym to tone her body (the cerebellum is responsible for maintaining muscle tone), and then she goes to school to teach motor activities (imagine her teaching the kids to drive!), and finally coordinates speech, posture, and movement (always telling kids to stand up straight and be quiet). With this easy-to-remember story, you've nailed down the name, location, and function of this brain region, with plenty of "handles" to jog your memory when needed.

Stories can be a great way to incorporate not just procedural or ordered information (first this happened, then this happened) but also capture information about relationships, motivations, connections, and cause and effect. If something seems dry or boring, make it into a character. Tell a goofy story—or imagine that the ideas fit into a pre-existing story that you couldn't forget if you tried. You wouldn't be the first person who tried to memorize boring WWII history by imagining the different parties as warring houses in Game of Thrones!

Technique 4: Mix Up Your Locations

Yes, we did drive home the point about setting up a proper work/study station with a distraction-free desk. Yes, it is important to have a routine and a dedicated space to work. However, there is also something to be said for varying the location of your studying as much as is feasible. This works for the same reason that creating rich and varied stimuli makes things easier to remember—there are more associations.

The more connections you make, the better. Perhaps you've already experienced this before: you recall a particular piece of information and cannot help also recalling the place and time in the past when you first encountered that information. Or, perhaps you go to a specific location and are suddenly reminded of a whole avalanche of memories that are seemingly triggered by simply being there.

Your location is simply more mental "scaffolding" onto which to build and cement new connections. At the time of studying, maybe you were deeply immersed in the moment and recall the birds singing outside, what you were wearing, and the time of day. In an exam the following day, closing your eyes to recall that birdsong and all the feelings associated with that moment, your brain helpfully produces the information you were studying as part of the scene.

To incorporate this idea into your own study schedule, try to switch up your study locations. Move to another room whenever you change chapter or section. The variations should be across all your senses—different sights, sounds, textures, smells, times of day, mood, and so on. You might even find it helpful to explicitly draw meaningful connections between the room you're in and the material you're studying.

Alternatively, study the same piece of material in many different locations. This is made extra powerful if you use mnemonics, imagery, or narrative that connects somehow with that place or your state of mind inside it. You could do your preparation in one room, then review in another room, then finally do worked examples or mock tests in a third room. If you have access to a library or local coffee shop, give these a try too—the former if you work better in complete silence, and the latter if you're one of those who works best when there's a low-level buzz around you.

If you can't realistically move from room to room, try to emphasize other smaller "scene changes" that will register in your brain, like moving to another chair in the room, getting up to walk around as you recite or memorize, or having a snack or particular (non-distracting) music playing in the background as you read. At the very least, change up your posture, the stationery you're using, the direction you're facing, or the style of study you're doing. For example, if your attention is flagging after thirty minutes on a written exercise, stop and switch to a video or audio recording to change things up and keep you motivated.

Technique 5: Give Yourself Time to Digest

A good rule of thumb is to "restore before more." Your brain is truly miraculous in its ability to absorb and retain, but its powers are not infinite—at some point, you need to rest and recuperate. Rest, as we've already seen, is really non-negotiable. It's not "down-time" but rather time spent consolidating, processing, and re-building up energy and cognitive resources for the next bout of study. Scrimp on rest time and you seriously compromise your memory and your learning efficiency.

Something you might not know is that having a sleep *immediately after* a study session can actually improve your recall of that material. A 2006 study by Gais et. al. showed that student subjects were able to remember far more vocabulary words from a list if they took a nap after memorizing, compared to others who didn't get the extra snooze time.

Sleep deprivation can certainly interfere with your brain's ability to put down and cement new neural connections, but it turns out that heading off to sleep after a challenging study session actually helps your brain "bank" what it's learned. If you can, schedule a study session a few hours before you go to sleep in the evenings—you have a few hours' wiggle room, and obviously don't need to try to study when you're really sleepy and exhausted from a long day. But this trick can be great when you're tackling something especially difficult. Not only will your brain get the chance to sort through the new material while you sleep, you'll be more refreshed after your sleep and ready to tackle the next step, having firmly consolidated the previous one.

One thing you can do is finish your study session with a summary or review (you should be doing this anyway) and then immediately review this again in the morning when you wake up. You may be surprised to see just how much easier and clearer things seem to you after a good night's sleep! Another idea is to tackle just one very difficult problem or concept, then head to bed and literally "sleep on it," checking to see if it makes more sense in the light of morning!

A similar study done by James T. Haynes IV had test participants doing a fifteen minute treadmill walk before sitting down to a study session. Those who walked before studying had better recall for a list of words than those who didn't. Chances are, you're already doing a walk or some form of exercise during the day; this is just a question of scheduling it optimally. You could eat your evening meal, take a short walk to help with digestion, then settle down for a study session, and then finally go to sleep a few hours later.

You don't necessarily have to go to bed to have a rest. Your brain may be completely burnt out, but you can still take a break by switching to a different task entirely—for example, one that is very physically demanding. You may even find that it's relatively relaxing to do something like deep clean the kitchen or get engrossed in a DIY project—your brain gets the chance to completely switch off and recover.

At any rate, if you notice that you're feeling extremely tired or sleepy during your study period, it's probably wise to just stop. Rest, take a walk, or do some stretches to get the blood flowing, have a healthy snack and a glass of water, or do some other task that doesn't require much mental effort. Return to your studies and see if you're still having trouble concentrating. If you are, you might consider scheduling that block to a time when you're more energetic, or asking whether you're getting enough sleep generally.

Technique 6: Chunking

This is a simple but powerful technique that you're probably already using without knowing it. The principle is simple: it's easier to remember small things than big things, so if you have a big thing to remember, just break it down into small pieces and remember those instead. Chunking is what it sounds like—organizing data into chunks or groups. Chunks are easier to remember. If you have to remember a shopping list, it will be far easier to remember that you have three things that go in salad, four things that begin with P, and two things that are pink. So, instead of remembering nine separate items, you remember only three groups.

Another example is to look for patterns in your study material, and group people, events, or concepts according to some bigger overarching principle. Then, you only have to remember the principle, which will in turn make it easier to remember the items you've put into that group. This is especially true if the principle makes a kind of common sense, meaning it's easier to recall. You could group elements on the periodic table according to their atomic number or some other criteria like color, clump together different kinds of historical monarchs and rulers according to their style of governance, or group truly random items into a list based on purely arbitrary similarities, such as whether you like them or not!

Most of us have a relatively fixed number of items we can recall without difficulty—you can test this yourself by seeing just how long a string of random digits you can remember. In 1956, Harvard professor George Miller published a paper titled *The Magical Number Seven, Plus or Minus Two; Some Limits on Our Capacity for Processing Information.* He found that humans could store around seven pieces of information in working memory at one go. However, these seven pieces can be chunked pieces, effectively expanding our inborn limits.

For example, consider the phone number (719) 455-2000. There are ten digits, but people can easily memorize this number if they remember the dialing code chunk (which might be the same as theirs) and think of the final four digits as one number—two thousand. In this way, they only have to remember essentially five pieces of information, not ten.

It's important to realize that chunking is *not* the same as simply dividing things up into categories and subcategories. Remember that your brain understands pictures, meaning, connections, and narratives. The principles by which you create categories and chunks have to make meaningful sense. It genuinely has to feel like you are condensing a bigger number of items into a smaller number, or else you may actually be giving yourself more work to do!

In a way, creating chunks is a little like *conceptual* mnemonics—in a mnemonic or acronym, each letter comes to stand in for some longer word. In the same way, when you make chunks, each chunk is a shorter and simplified symbol that comes to stand in for longer or more complex pieces of information. You remember only these shorthand cues, which then allow you to index information away and, in effect, store way more and with less effort.

Technique 7: Spaced Repetition

This method is directly aimed at dealing with beating forgetting . . . which is a little like being better at remembering! Spaced repetition—otherwise known as distributed practice—is just what it sounds like. You are essentially making sure you have ample opportunity to practice what matters: recall. Practice makes perfect, and this is true for memory, too. The more you retrieve a memory, the easier it becomes to retrieve it. Simple, really!

The reason it is such an important technique in improving your memory is that it battles forgetting directly and allows you to work within the bounds of your brain's capabilities. Other techniques, no less important, are about increasing encoding or storage—remember, the three parts of memory are encoding, storage, and retrieval. Spaced repetition helps the last part—retrieval.

In order to commit more to memory and retain information better, space out your rehearsal and exposure to it over as long of a period as possible. In other words, you will remember something far better if you study it for one hour a day versus twenty hours in one weekend. This goes for just about everything you could possibly learn. Additional research has shown that seeing something twenty times in one day is far less effective than seeing something ten times over the course of seven days.

Spaced repetition makes more sense if you imagine your brain as a muscle. Muscles can't be exercised all the time and then put back to work with little-to-no recovery. Your brain needs time to make connections between concepts, create muscle memory, and generally become familiar with something. Sleep has been shown to be where neural connections are made, and it's not just mental. Synaptic connections are formed in your brain, and dendrites are stimulated.

If an athlete works out too hard in one session like you might be tempted to in studying, one of two things will happen. The athlete will either be too exhausted and the latter half of the workout will be useless, or the athlete will become injured. Rest and recovery are necessary to the task of learning, and sometimes effort isn't what's required.

Here's a look at what a schedule focused on spaced repetition might look like.

Monday at 10:00 a.m. Learn initial facts about Spanish history. You accumulate five pages of notes.

Monday at 8:00 p.m. Review notes about Spanish history, but don't just review passively. Make sure to try to recall the information from your own memory. Recalling is a much better way to process information than simply rereading and reviewing. This might only take twenty minutes.

Tuesday at 10:00 a.m. Try to recall the information without looking at your notes much. After you first try to actively recall as much as possible, go back through your notes to see what you missed, and make note of what you need to pay closer attention to. This will probably take only fifteen minutes.

Tuesday at 8:00 p.m. Review notes. This will take ten minutes.

Wednesday at 4:00 p.m. Try to independently recall the information again, and only look at your notes once you are done to see what else you have missed. This will take only ten minutes. Make sure not to skip any steps.

Thursday at 6:00 p.m. Review notes. This will take ten minutes.

Friday at 10:00 a.m. Active recall session. This will take ten minutes.

Looking at this schedule, note that you are only studying an additional seventy-five minutes throughout the week, but that you've managed to go through the entire lesson a whopping six additional times. Not only that, you've likely committed most of it to memory because you are using active recall instead of passively reviewing your notes.

You're ready for a test the next Monday. Actually, you're ready for a test by Friday afternoon. Spaced repetition gives your brain time to process concepts and make its own connections and leaps because of the repetition.

Think about what happens when you have repeated exposure to a concept. For the first couple exposures, you may not see anything new. As you get more familiar with it and stop going through the motions, you begin to examine it on a deeper level and think about the context surrounding it. You relate it to other concepts or information, and you generally make sense of it below surface level.

All of this, of course, is designed to push information from your short-term memory into your long-term memory. That's why cramming or studying at the last minute isn't an effective means of learning. Very little tends to make it into long-term memory because of the lack of repetition and deeper analysis. At that point, it becomes rote memorization instead of the concept learning we discussed earlier, which is destined to fade far more quickly.

When you set out to learn something, instead of measuring the number of hours you spend on something, try instead to measure the number of times you revisit the same information after the initial learning. Make it your goal to increase the frequency of reviewing, not necessarily the duration. Both matter, but the literature on spaced repetition or distributed practice makes clear that breathing room is necessary.

It's true that this type of optimal learning takes up more time and planning than most of us are used to. However, if you find yourself short on time, you can still use it strategically.

To cram for a test, exam, or other type of evaluation, we don't need material to make it to our long-term memory. We just need it to make it slightly past our working memory and be partially encoded into our long-term memory. We don't need to be able to recall anything the day after, so it's like we only need something to stick for a few hours.

You might not be able to do true spaced repetition if you are cramming at the last minute, but you can simulate it in a small way. Instead of studying subject X for three hours only at night, seek to study it one hour each three times a day with a few hours between each exposure.

Recall that memories need time to be encoded and stick in the brain. You are doing the best imitation of spaced repetition you can with what you have available. To get the most out of your limited studying time, study something, for example, as soon as you wake up, and then review it at noon, 4:00 p.m., and 9:00 p.m. The point is to review throughout the day and get as much repetition as possible. Remember to focus on frequency rather than duration.

During the course of your repetition, make sure to study your notes out of order to see them in different contexts and encode more effectively. Also, use active recall versus passive reading. Don't be afraid to even intersperse unrelated material to reap the benefits of interleaved practice. Make sure to focus on the underlying concepts that govern the information you are learning so you can make educated guesses about what you don't remember.

Make sure that you're reciting and rehearsing new information up to the last minute before your test. Your short-term memory can hold seven items on its best day, so you might just save yourself with a piece of information that was never going to fit into your long-term memory. It's like you're juggling. It's inevitable that you'll drop everything, but it could just so happen that you're juggling something you can use. Make use of all types of memory you can consciously employ.

Spaced repetition, as you can see, approaches learning from a different perspective—in practicing retrieval and shooting for frequency as opposed to duration to improve memory. Even in situations where you don't have as much time as you'd like, you can use spaced repetition to cram for tests and overall just get more information into your brain— again, by focusing on frequency and not duration. When you spread out your learning and memorizing over a longer period of time and revisit the same material frequently, you'll be better off.

Technique 8: Practice Testing and Retrieval Practice

Finally, there is one major technique that applies the fickle nature of memory: *retrieval practice.*

We typically consider learning as something we absorb—something that goes *into* our brains: the teacher or textbook spits facts, data, equations, and words out at us, and we just sit there and collect them. It's merely accumulation—a very *passive* act.

This kind of relationship with learning returns knowledge that we don't retain for very long because, even though we *get* it, we don't *do* much with it. For best results, we have to make learning an *active* operation.

That's where retrieval practice comes into play. Instead of putting more stuff *in* our brains, retrieval practice helps us take knowledge *out* of our brains and put it to use. That seemingly small change in thinking dramatically improves our chances of retaining and remembering what we learn. Everyone remembers flashcards from childhood days. The fronts of the cards had math equations, words, science terms, or images, and the backs had the "answer"— the solution, definition, explanation, or whatever response the student is expected to give.

The idea of flashcards sprouts from a strategy called *retrieval practice*. This approach is neither new nor very complicated: it's simply recalling information you've already learned (the back of the flashcard) when prompted by a certain image or depiction (the front).

Retrieval practice is one of the best ways to increase your memory and fact retention. But even though its core is quite simple, actually using retrieval practice isn't quite as straightforward as just passively drilling with flashcards or scanning over notes we've taken. Rather, retrieval practice is an active skill: truly struggling, thinking, and processing to finally get to the point of recalling that information without clues— much of what we've discussed already in this book that accelerates learning.

Pooja Agarwal researched pupils taking middle school social studies over the course of a year and a half, ending in 2011. The study aimed to determine how regularly scheduled, uncounted quizzes—basically, retrieval practice exercises—benefitted the ability to learn and retain.

The class teacher didn't alter their study plan and simply instructed as normal. The students were given regular quizzes—developed by the research team—on class material with the understanding that the results would *not* count against their grades.

These quizzes only included about a third of the material covered by the teacher, who also had to leave the room while the quiz was being taken. This was so the teacher had no knowledge of what subjects the quizzes covered. During class, the teacher taught and reviewed the class as usual, without knowing which parts of the instruction were being asked on the quizzes.

The results of this study were measured during end-of-unit exams and were quite dramatic. Students scored one full grade level higher on the material the quizzes covered—the one-third of what the whole class covered—than the questions *not* asked on the no-stakes quizzes. The mere act of being occasionally tested, with no pressure to get all the answers right to boost their overall grades, actually helped students learn better.

Agarwal's study also provided insight on what kind of questions helped the most. Questions that required the student to actually recall the information from scratch yielded more success than multiple-choice questions, in which the answer could be recognized from a list, or true/false questions. The active mental effort to remember the answer with no verbal or visual prompt improved the students' learning and retention.

Using Retrieval Practice in Our Lives

The principal benefit of retrieval practice is that it encourages an *active* exertion of effort rather than the passive seepage of external information. When we learn something once and then actually *do* something else to reinforce our learning, it has more of an effect than merely reviewing notes or re-reading passages in books.

The knowledge that we store in our memory is activated when it's called out. Retrieval practice stimulates that movement and makes it easier to learn and retain new understandings. If we pull concepts *out* of our brain, it's more effective than just continually trying to put concepts *in*. The learning comes from taking what's been added to our knowledge and bringing it out at a later time.

We mentioned flashcards at the top of this section and how they're an offshoot of retrieval practice. But flashcards are not, in and of themselves, the strategy: you *can* use them and still not be conducting true retrieval practice.

Many students use flashcards somewhat inactively: they see the prompt, answer it in their heads, tell themselves they know it, flip over to see the answer, and then move on to the next one. Turning this into *practice*, however, would be taking a few seconds to actually recall the answer and, at best, say the answer out loud before flipping the card over. The difference seems slight and subtle, but it's important. Students will get more advantages from flashcards by actually retrieving and vocalizing the answer before moving on.

In real-world situations—where there's usually not an outside teacher, premade flashcards, or other assistance—how can we repurpose what we learn for retrieval practice? One good way is to expand flashcards to make them more "interactive."

The flashcards in our grade-school experiences, for the most part, were very one-note. You can adapt the methodology of flashcards for more complex, real-world applications or self-learning by taking a new approach to what's on the back of the cards, as suggested by writer Rachel Adragna.

When you're studying material for work or class, make flashcards with concepts on the front and definitions on the back. After completing this task, make another set of cards that give "instructions" on how to reprocess the concept for a creative or real-life situation. Here's an example:

- "Rewrite this concept in plain English."

- "Write a movie or novel plot that demonstrates this concept."

- "Use this concept to describe a real-life event."

- "Describe the *opposite* of this concept."

- "Draw a picture of this concept."

The possibilities are, as they say, limitless in how you can seek retrieval. Using these exercises extracts more information about the concept that you produce yourself. Placing them in the context of a creative narrative or expression will help you understand them when they come up in real life. Our memories are fickle, and they like to play tricks on us by design, but they can be molded to our advantage in learning more quickly.

Takeaways

- Knowing how to stretch your memory to its full potential is a big part of mastering your chosen subject and acing exams. The brain has natural limits, but if you know how to work around them, you can learn to remember more.

- One technique is to convert information to images or nonverbal data, which is easier to remember. Try mind maps or concept maps, diagrams, flowcharts, or other visualizations.

- Mnemonics are memory devices that make memorizing facts easier. The best mnemonics are those that are personally relevant, make meaningful sense to you, and are relevant to the material somehow.

- The brain is always looking for connections and relationships, so draw on this tendency by presenting new material in the form of a story. Make it colorful, humorous, personally relevant, or even a little rude—it's all easier to remember.

- Though study strategies are important, it's essential to have enough down time so your brain can rest, recuperate, and consolidate the new material it's taken in. It may be worth scheduling study sessions so you can sleep immediately afterward, especially if you tackled challenging material. Alternatively, switch tasks to help you turn off for a while.

- Use the power of chunking to reduce the cognitive load on your brain, i.e. the amount of information it has to work to store. Organize many smaller pieces of information into chunks, which are then more easily recalled. The brain can hold approximately seven pieces of information in the working memory at one time, but a "cheat code" is to fold and nest smaller items so that you're effectively remembering far more than seven. As with other techniques, make sure your chunks make sense and are relevant to you to increase your chances of recall.

- Spaced repetition is the practice of frequent recall to combat forgetting. The trick is to space out repeated exposures over a long period and rehearse little and often, rather than cramming.

- Practice testing and retrieval practice is practice that focuses on active, productive memory—it's about *doing* something with the material, thereby embedding it more solidly.
- Each of these memory techniques is best used in conjunction. The more the merrier—combine them in colorful, creative ways and you increase the neural connections you build and ensure that the memory is firmly stored for later retrieval.

Chapter 5. Exam Day Strategies

Have a Plan, Come Prepared

When you study, you need a plan, and when you turn up on the day to write your exam, you *definitely* need a plan. This is especially true if you're one of those people who genuinely understands their work, yet somehow their grades never truly reflect it. Running out of time, "freezing," and forgetting everything you know, or wasting too much time on the wrong question—all these mistakes can throw all your hard work out the window and leave you with a bad grade.

You need a strategy. We'll outline one here, but remember that it's up to you to tweak and refine it to best match your needs with your particular study situation.

Step 1: Prepare

If you've been diligently planning a study schedule and sticking to it, you'll naturally feel ready and less stressed. No matter how tempting it seems, don't cram the day before. In fact, go easy and spend the day revising and getting in the right frame of mind. Get a good nights' sleep, eat well, stay hydrated, and make sure that everything is lined up to run smoothly, i.e. you've set your alarm, laid out your clothing for the day, know where you're going and what time, and have packed a bag with everything you need. Before an exam, you need to *relax*. And to do this, you need to make sure you have everything you need and won't be rushed or distracted.

Step 2: Read Well and Orient

Okay, take a deep breath, here's the paper. First, just read it through front to back. If you've done plenty of practice or past papers, you'll probably recognize the format as well as the content. That's great—but try to avoid making assumptions *and read the damn question!*

This is important. You'll forget it in the heat of the moment, but consciously remind yourself: *read the damn question!* You never think that you'd read the question wrong or misunderstand what you've been asked. But yes, it happens, and it even happens to the best of us. There's no doubt that getting crystal clear on the question is the lowest-hanging fruit. It's so easy to confirm and get right, but if you get it wrong, it's so easy to lose an enormous number of marks.

Read through the entire paper and then re-read each individual question. This is not wasted time, but a valuable strategy for orienting yourself and focusing your limited time and attention as efficiently as possible.

Read through the paper and look at the mark allocation for each question. You might like to note which ones you know the answers to already, as well as the questions that are worth the most points. Accordingly, plan the order you'll write the paper, beginning with those easy points to get them in the bag. You don't want to angst over the difficult question and run out of time for the question you actually would have gotten right.

For each individual question, read it through slowly and think carefully what you are being asked to produce and how. Look at the mark allocation and imagine the points the rubric will be looking to award points for. Make sure you're not getting led astray by tricky phrasing luring you into answering in a way that completely misses the point. Look at the verbs for a clue on what you're expected to do, and ask what form your answer must take and its length.

Step 3: Budget Your Time

Let's say you have three hours to write a paper, with fifty percent of the marks coming from a multiple-choice section, twenty-five percent from a long or essay question, and twenty-five percent from a diagram-drawing question. Logic suggests you spend around one and a half hours on the multiple choice, but let's say that you've read through everything and you predict you'll struggle with the diagram, but the multiple choice questions all look easy.

In this case, you might decide to budget less time for the multiple choice questions, but do them first, and then give yourself more time to do the diagram, but tackle it last once you know you've bagged as many marks as possible for the other sections. You could quickly scribble a mini-schedule for yourself—noting the times to stop and start on each new section. This will stop you from running out of time and help you feel a bit more in control.

Step 4: Begin

Now, start with those easy wins you identified. Depending on the form of the question, you could possibly jot down some notes or outlines on a spare piece of paper to structure your thoughts, write down acronyms/mnemonics, or plan an essay. Exactly how you answer the question will depend heavily on the topic, the form of the test and the level of the material. But here are some general tips to keep in mind:

- In math and science papers, pay close attention to your units. Read what units are presented in the question and what unit you're asked to present your answer. Do you need to do any conversions? Don't lose marks by not giving final answers with the full and correct units, i.e. m s^2.

- For math papers, show your work and be as clear and precise as possible

- For any scientific or technical subject, double check your answers to see if they make everyday sense. If you're calculating the volume of a fishbowl, for example, and you get 4.5 nanoliters, you've probably messed up somewhere!

- For drawing graphs or diagrams, make sure you always add titles, label axes, and include units.

- For any calculation or problem, write on the one side of the question what is given or known, and what you are being asked to calculate. It helps!

- For essay-style questions, make sure that each paragraph is addressing only one point, which is covered succinctly in a topic sentence. Plan your central argument out first, making sure that you're approaching the topic in the way the question has stipulated.

- Sounds unimportant, but write neatly! You'll slow down and be more methodical, plus your work will be more legible.

Step 5: Check . . . and Check Again

Proceed through all the questions according to their difficulty and the mini-schedule you made for yourself. If necessary, you may have to adjust this or (if you're lucky) find you have extra time. Either way, monitor your progress and keep an eye on how much time you have. Once you've completed an answer, pause, then read over the question and answer again, looking for any errors or omissions. Look for obvious things—like a missing minus sign or a silly confusion of similar terms.

How much should you check? There's no point getting obsessive or superstitious. Do what you can, check a few times, then move confidently on. Forget any nonsense about "going with your gut feeling" on questions or changing your answer at the last minute—you'll drive yourself crazy. Close your paper and tell yourself that you have done everything you can, and that you are finished now. You'll know your grade soon enough, but right now, it's out of your hands, and it's no use stressing about it at all.

Multiple Choice Strategy

Let's take a closer look at a very common exam question format: multiple choice. You always have chance on your side, which can make the exam feel a little less stressful. This is one format that really benefits from a solid strategy since you *know*, buried somewhere in there, is the right answer, and all you have to do is dig it out! Here's a strategy for doing the digging.

Step 1: Read

Same as other questions—read! Look at verbs to tell you what you're being asked to do, and watch out for negative phrasing like *not* or *none*, or absolute terms like *never*. Multiple choice questions can be surprisingly difficult, especially if they contain options like "both a and b" or "neither b nor c" and so on.

For more difficult questions, underline key words and terms, and potentially rewrite them in your own vocabulary if it helps you better grasp the concept. Identify bits of information you know are irrelevant, red herrings, or there to distract you.

A good idea is to read just the question first and see if you can find the answer without looking at the answers. Then peek at the answers and see if it's there . . .

Step 2: Cull the Obviously Incorrect Options

Before you choose that answer, though, look at the other options. There isn't always one, but if you *absolutely know* an answer is not correct, scratch that off the list. Be careful that you haven't been tricked (you've already read and re-read the question, right?) and then move on.

Step 3: Look at very Similar Answers

Now to whittle things down further. Are there any options that are very similar to one another? Tease out which one is right. Think about what their similarity is telling you about the question itself, and what you're being asked to know and prove in this question. For example, if the answers are all the same figure but with different units, you obviously know that you need to pay special attention to units as you figure the answer out.

Sometimes, the way the questions and answers are framed in itself gives you clues about how to solve the problem. Let's say you look at one option and you know it's false. What's the opposite of this statement, and can you find something that looks like that in the answers? You might not be able to decide which is the right answer, in which case think about which is the worst one and work by elimination. It's occasionally possible to eliminate answers just given the differences in language or logic between the question and answer.

Step 4: Make a Choice

The biggest risk with multiple choice is that you quickly choose something that seems right instead of methodically considering each answer on its own merits. Make a choice only *after* you've thoroughly chewed over all the options. What if you encounter a question that you just don't know the answer to?

If you are not penalized for incorrect answers, you'll have to guess. Eliminate what you can and then choose. Examine the format and style of previous questions you know you've gotten correct, and see if you can infer anything about those questions you're stumped on. For example, if you notice that the right answer is often the last one, or the longest and most detailed one, then factor that into your guess. You could also eliminate what you can and then return to the question later without dwelling on it. You may be surprised by how your unconscious mind works on the problem in the background, and that you may feel more confident when you return to it later!

Step 5: Review

If you've done the steps above as thoroughly as you can, there isn't much to review, but nevertheless, it's worth checking once more to see if you've done what you can within the allotted time you've given yourself for each question. Though it's possible to wrangle a few more points by doing creative guesswork, try not to waste too much time or energy on this unless you finish early. You may be able to get some clues from other questions, but avoid last-minute changes on blind faith or a hunch!

Essay Question Strategy

Next, we'll look at essay questions. These are, in a way, a lot more challenging than multiple choice questions, but students needn't worry since they can do a lot to prepare ahead of time to ensure they write a great essay. Past papers can give you a good idea of the kind of topic question you can expect, and lecturers/teachers often give big hints allowing you to predict the scope and kind of question you'll get. This means you can practice ahead of time and prepare a few model answers for essays you're most likely to have to produce in an exam.

Unlike multiple choice, you earn most of your essay exam question points in the time *before* the exam, when you prepare.

Step 1: Anticipate and Prepare

Look at previous questions on past exams. Look at their format and how they were phrased. Will you be asked to compare or contrast ideas, make an original argument, or critically analyze a situation given some theory? Look at the big ideas of the course you're studying and the main skills your lecturers want to see you demonstrate. Try to predict what higher-order tasks you'll have to show, and prepare accordingly.

Step 2: Do Test Runs

Write a few possible test questions and then, for each one, compile a short summary and outline for how you would answer that question. Lay out the overall structure of the essay with the points you can cover in each paragraph or section. For now, just have bullet points or key concepts.

Identify any key facts, events, or bits of data you need to memorize to write these essays well, and make sure you're studying and drilling those separately. When you've done this, you might like to choose a few (as many as you have time for, really) and write a full essay from it within the time limit. Recreate the exam conditions and see how well you do. You could even mark your own paper to see if you can spot any weak points or things to improve on.

Step 3: Outline

In the exam itself, read through the question clearly and orient yourself. Then, do a "brain dump" where you jot down everything you can think of that relates to the topic. Next, chart out a plan and structure for how you'll arrange this information into a form to address the question. If you're asked to compare two models, you might decide to spend two paragraphs on one model, two on the other, and then three paragraphs directly comparing them.

You could draw a quick table to briefly list their differences and make sure you're including each point. Now's the time to decide how many words you can allocate to each point. Spend some time making sure that each of these points actually flows logically into the other to form an argument. Good essays contain three things: a thesis (your main point), evidence to support that thesis, and a logical and coherent flow between those pieces of evidence. So, it's not just about what you know, but how you can connect it all and present it in one complete case.

Step 4: Write the Essay

The essay question should not seem like a surprise to you. Even if you forget a few key details, remember that you get points for properly structuring your argument and addressing the question. Once you've outlined, dive in and write.

A few essay rules of thumb:

- If appropriate, it's usually worth including brief definitions of theories or concepts
- Start the essay with background or framing context, or a brief overview of the problem at hand
- One point per paragraph with a consistent structure; for example, each paragraph consisting of a topic sentence followed by evidence or elaboration, plus something to link and transition to the next paragraph
- Include an introduction and a conclusion, but actually synthesize rather than merely repeating or listing. Show your marker that you have a single, focused point you're making
- Try to avoid regurgitating the essay you've practiced at home, whether it fits the question or not
- Leave generous space between paragraphs as you write—you may want to squeeze in a sentence or two at the last minute

- As always, double check for spelling, grammar, and punctuation errors
- Try to use the same terms and vocabulary in the question itself in your essay. Make sure that you're addressing *all* parts of the question and not just one
- Keep things neatly written, formal, and concise. Double check that you're not including unnecessary info that adds nothing to your main point.
- Keep your eye on your time limit! When you pad out answers, waffle, or bluff, you actually only waste time and earn no extra points. Save your writing muscles and just move on
- On that note, don't be tempted to add in literally anything you can think of on the topic. Teachers won't give you points for including correct but irrelevant info. Be ruthless—does it answer the question and is it really relevant?
- Read through the essay when you're done to make any last minute tweaks

Conduct an Exam Postmortem

Hooray! You've gotten through your exams, you've received your grades, and now it's time to put your feet up and relax. Well done.

In a way, though, your most important work as a student is only just beginning . . .

It might be the last thing you feel like doing, but right now, you have the precious opportunity of seeing just how well your study method actually worked. Armed with this knowledge, you can adjust and tweak your approach so that next time, you're even better. Ask yourself seriously—have you been approaching every new exam in exactly the same way as you did the one before, regardless of whether these techniques actually worked or not? If most of us are honest, when it comes to studying, we tend to just keep on doing the same thing over and over again, never really stopping to question the effectiveness of our approach.

Consider it this way: learning is a question of *adaptation*. Unless you are able to clearly see how you've performed and adjust yourself accordingly, you never really learn or grow, and never become better. You just stay where you are. Many people have a strange relationship to "failure." Perhaps they treat it as something shameful, or a mistake that needs to be forgotten and moved past as soon as possible.

But failing is not a mistake—it's a necessary step on the path to learning. If you don't address and correct errors, they simply embed themselves and become more permanent. You've probably been looking at past exam papers and looking over sample questions and problems, and this is extremely useful. But the value is not in anticipating what the exam will be so you can parrot what you've memorized and then forget it immediately after. Rather, these practice tests are an opportunity to uncover your own misunderstandings, your own gaps in understanding, and the areas where you most need to improve.

It's tempting to shrink away from the extra difficult, confusing things that we always get wrong, but think of it this way—these are the low-hanging fruit, and you have the *greatest potential* for improvement if you work on these. After all, how much better can you get at something that you're already pretty good at? But work on your tricky areas and you do something special—you learn and improve.

In this final section, we're looking at a commonly ignored part of the learning process, i.e. everything that happens *after* the exam is written and marked. In the exam, wouldn't you have given anything to see what errors you were making? Well, doing an exam "post-mortem" is the next best thing and gives you insight that you can then feed back into your next study session.

You don't have to wait until after your exams to make use of this iterative process, though. You can always test yourself, observe your performance, ask what went wrong, and fix it. You can repeat this process as often as you like before the real exam. Whether you are able to pick apart an actual exam you've done in the past or have to test yourself and analyze your answers, there's a knack to identifying your errors. What *type* of error have you made?

Types of Errors

Type 1: Errors of Omission

Something that should be there isn't there. You've missed important content somewhere along the line. Perhaps you're very familiar with your work but there's a big black gap around a certain chapter or concept. Maybe you've missed an important class or overlooked some information. If you've lost marks for simply not including something that should have been included, then ask yourself why that happened.

Did you misunderstand the scope of the paper? Have you missed lectures or modules? Is there some other reason why you've avoided, neglected, or forgotten to include certain topics? Fix the problem by focusing intently on these areas in the future, and commit to tightening up your schedule if you've been careless or disorganized. Make sure that you're crystal clear on the scope of your study and are including *everything*.

Type 2: Careless Errors

It's not that you don't know the work or have a deep, fundamental misunderstanding. You just made a silly mistake, like misreading the question, accidentally forgetting that there were questions printed on the other side of the paper, or running out of time because your watch was slow.

If you've made a careless mistake, what really caused it? Chances are you were feeling rushed, distracted, or anxious. Anything that interferes with your calm, focused attention is going to increase your chances of making an avoidable mistake. The solution is simple: next time round, make sure that you're breathing, staying calm, and budgeting your time properly so you don't have to rush.

Slow down—the irony is that rushing to finish can have you making errors that actually take more time to fix. Be prepared and methodical. At the start of each new question, cover up all the other questions, take a deep breath, and just focus on what's in front of you. Factor in enough time to check through everything at the end.

Type 3: Having the Wrong Priorities

You turn up to the exam and realize that you spent hours and hours studying something that isn't tested at all. Or there are questions on what you studied, but you find out you went into way too much (or too little!) detail, completely misunderstanding how seriously you were meant to take certain aspects of the course work. Or, worst of all, you consciously disregarded certain content only to find it heavily focused on in the paper, and then you fail.

In the rush to get studying as soon as possible and get the hours in, we can make an error early on when we decide what is and what isn't relevant to study. We might make an assumption about what the focus of the exam will be, or decide to "spot study" and predict what will be tested so we can only study that material.

This is a massive problem that can be avoided relatively easily. No, you don't have to "study the test," but you should make sure you have a clear idea of the examinable component *before* you start making your study plan. Ask your teachers or lecturers for some hints, or failing that, past papers and prior exams give you a good idea of the relative proportion of the different topics. It's not rocket science; if there are repeated overlapping concepts, these are likely to be important in the exam, whereas optional assigned readings or supplemental materials are not likely to be a core focus.

Type 4: Errors in Application

Maybe you diligently memorized a list of items but then were completely stumped when you were asked to connect them in some way. Maybe you learned all the facts and details, but are now faced with a question that is asking you to apply those ideas to a completely novel situation. When we study, we necessarily take things apart into chapters, sections, topics. But often we'll be asked to put it all back together again and present some meaningful, coherent picture of how they all fit together.

The trick here is to understand the question format you'll likely have in the exam, and understand not just *what* your examiners are asking for but *how* you can demonstrate that knowledge so they can award marks. It's usually not good enough to just absorb data; you need to be able to show that you can analyze it, rephrase it, and synthesize it into something different. So, if this is an error you make frequently, you may need to try to make concept maps rather than simple factual mind maps, or start your study session by asking, "What's the big idea here? What is the relationship/connection between all these disparate elements?"

Type 5: Mastery Errors

If you frequently make this kind of error, you can probably tell. This is when you don't really understand the material that well or have big gaps in your understanding that make it hard to answer the question completely. You might even have difficulties getting why you were wrong in the first place after seeing the correct answers. This is a sure sign that, to put it bluntly, you're not quite there yet.

Whether you lack the knowledge or skills outright or whether you're simply unable to go into the depth required, the solution is to head back to the drawing board and try again. You may have underestimated how much time and effort were required, or may need to ramp up your efforts to get extra help on those concepts you're struggling with.

Sometimes, markers can be a little unfair and grade you down even when your answer is sufficient, so make sure this isn't the case before worrying that you haven't properly mastered the material. In this case, it may be more a matter of learning to better communicate what you know and present it in a way that is most accessible to the teachers marking the paper.

As you go through your marked work, ask yourself a few questions to shape your strategy next time round:

- How accurate was your prediction about what the exam would be like? Did you make any assumptions about the style or material that were in hindsight unfounded? What have you learned about the exam format?
- What kind of mistakes did you make and what do they say about your current grasp of the material?
- What concrete steps can you take right now to ensure that you're less likely to make those mistakes again?
- Finally, ask what you did *right*. Look at what you managed successfully and ask why. Now you have evidence that this approach yields results—so keep it up!

Having a good mastery over your topic is one thing, but it's another thing entirely to master the exam process itself. You want to make sure you know the material inside and out, but you also have to understand *how* you'll make sure all that knowledge and skill is showing up on that all-important exam day. You have to learn to organize and synthesize what you know so that you can properly communicate it on the exam.

If you didn't do as well on an exam (or practice exam) as you hoped, don't despair. It can be really disappointing and upsetting if you had a lot riding on the result, but give yourself time to process these negative feelings before you look at your performance with a calm, neutral eye. Don't beat yourself up or start to feel avoidant or fatalistic about the subject entirely, but resist this temptation and appraise your performance like an investigator or scientist genuinely trying to understand what happened. You may discover that you haven't really made any "errors" as such, but rather that the exam was unusually hard, or that your expectations were perhaps too high. Maturing your perspective, too, is a part of becoming skillful not just with this single topic or single exam, but mastering the process of learning itself.

Takeaways

- Just as you need a strategy to tackle your exam schedule, you need one to tackle the exam itself on D Day. No two students will have the same strategy, but a good rule of thumb is to make sure you're prepared well ahead of time and that you make your first duty in the exam to read thoroughly and orient yourself before answering anything. Read the paper well to see what you know and which questions will be difficult.
- Before starting, budget your time carefully, taking into account any tricky areas as well as the mark allocation. Note down a mini-schedule and keep an eye on the time to make sure you're sticking to it. Then begin the paper.
- For technical or scientific exams, watch out for units or muddled terms. For other topics, make sure you're taking the time to plan out answers, keeping organized, and really read what you are being asked in the question.
- Multiple choice questions are easily done with the right strategy. As always, start by reading the questions thoroughly, then try to answer on your

own before reading the options. Use a process of elimination to delete obviously wrong answers, then work to discern between two or more very similar answers. Make your decision before a final check right at the end, but resist changing your answer at the last minute. At the very least, you have some non-zero chance of getting it right by accident!

- For essays, most of your success will come down to adequate prep beforehand. Start by anticipating the form and content of the essay question so you can prepare, and then get to work structuring and organizing material so you are ready to answer a range of possible questions. Create outlines for model answers and choose a few to write from scratch under exam conditions.

- Finally, learning doesn't stop after the exam is done. Use your results to help you identify where you've gone wrong, and feed that back into your strategy going forward. This is the essence of learning. Ask what type of error you've made, and commit to addressing it the next time round.

CHAPTER 1: MAKING THE MOST OF CLASSROOM TIME

- Making the most of your time in the classroom comes down to practicing active and focused listening. Listening is really a collection of many different competencies and happens along five stages.
- During the *reception stage*, we consciously pay attention to new material and make the effort to take it in. In the *understanding stage*, we take what we've heard and find its meaning and contextualize it, focusing on the purpose of the material and how it's relevant to us.
- In the *evaluating stage*, we consider our own personal evaluation of the material, its quality and application, and whether we agree or like what we've heard. In the *response stage*, we react to the information verbally or nonverbally.

Finally, during the *remembering stage*, we revisit what we've heard/learned and recall it with the use of cues to jog our memory.

- In reality, these stages overlap and blur into one another and repeat continually through the learning process. Problems at any stage can mean problems with truly grasping the material overall.

- The HEAR technique can help structure and guide your listening. First, halt (stop what you're doing and focus on what you hear), then engage (by taking notes, asking questions, or paraphrasing), anticipate (predict what will be said next and prepare for it), and replay (review what has been said to cement it in your mind).

- The Peter method of notetaking helps you really digest and *transform* material. There are four stages: normal detailed notetaking, summarizing that information in your own words and noting questions, connecting these ideas to the bigger picture, and summarizing each section to solidify and answer remaining questions. By systematically extracting and rewriting key info, you make your notetaking an active, intelligent process. The SQ3R is a way to process written texts, and consists of five steps: survey, question, read, recite, and review.

- Ultimately, when you can actively ask questions and think critically about the material, you have a better chance of understanding, memorizing, and mastering it.

CHAPTER 2: SUBJECT MASTERY

- By learning to teach others, we deepen our own understanding and retention, since we uncover a richer and more fundamental appreciation of the concepts behind the material. Compared to other strategies, teaching others may have the highest chance of improving recall and comprehension.
- The protégé effect is the observation that students who teach others do better, perhaps because they learn incrementally, take responsibility for the learning process, and are "ego-protected" from the prospect of failure.

- Analogies, examples, and metaphors are powerful tools to convey new concepts. To use them effectively in teaching/learning, make use of as many different analogies as possible and mix them in frequently, using examples to illustrate. Only use those analogies that actually work (i.e. don't forget their purpose) and reserve them more complex topics, since they may only confuse simpler ideas.

- Bloom's taxonomy is a roadmap to chart one's understanding and mastery of a topic. It can be used to identify the next step we need to take to deepen our grasp. Each step depends on mastery of the steps before it, although it's not necessary to achieve all stages.

- The stages are: remember, understand, apply, analyze, evaluate, and create. If you're struggling with the material, you can diagnose your position in the taxonomy and then attempt to overcome the obstacle by engaging with tasks from the next level. You can also avoid working at one level when you haven't achieved the previous ones—and confusing yourself further.

- Productive failure is the name given to mistakes, fumbling, or errors that actually illuminate our understanding better than simply being told the correct approach. Figuring things out for yourself can feel difficult in the moment, but it gives you a richer and more nuanced grasp of the material. The lesson is to embrace the learning curve, including mess ups and uncertainty, and use failure to drive understanding.

CHAPTER 3: MAKING A PLAN AND MANAGING YOUR TIME

- Effective studying is all about carefully managing your time and resources. It's also about making sure you set the stage for success and create an environment conducive to learning. Set up a comfortable, quiet, and distraction-free zone where you study.
- Decide what time of the day and week you'll study according to your own rhythms and preferences. Shorter, more frequent sessions are ideal, planned regularly when you're most energetic

and able to focus. Block out this time on a weekly schedule.

- Studying well is more of a long-term habit than an isolated event. Commit to designing a strategy that works for you. First, make a list that you follow every session to keep momentum.

- Make sure you're doing something to manage and contain stress and anxiety, such as meditation, journaling, or scheduling time to tackle fears and concerns without them jeopardizing your work.

- When you make your study plan, focus on two alternating components: preparation and review. In preparation, you generate unique and personal notes, summarize, organize concepts, and work through new ideas. In review, you consolidate what you've covered by testing yourself or doing worked examples. How much time you spend on each will depend on your topic and your level of mastery.

- Make sure you are regularly alternating these two aspects and mixing up both your prep and review portions with diversified approaches. The sooner you start, the sooner you can see what works and what doesn't and adjust accordingly.

- A lifestyle that supports learning is a healthy lifestyle; sleep enough, eat well, and consciously manage stress levels. Make sure you have regular rest periods to bank what you learn.

- There are some scientifically proven techniques for getting the most from your study sessions, including deep breathing, decluttering your workspace, keeping an optimal temperature, and making sure you never study in your bed.

CHAPTER 4: MEMORY TECHNIQUES

- Knowing how to stretch your memory to its full potential is a big part of mastering your chosen subject and acing exams. The brain has natural limits, but if you know how to work around them, you can learn to remember more.

- One technique is to convert information to images or nonverbal data, which is easier to remember. Try mind maps or concept maps, diagrams, flowcharts, or other visualizations.

- Mnemonics are memory devices that make memorizing facts easier. The best mnemonics are those that are personally relevant, make meaningful sense to you, and are relevant to the material somehow.

- The brain is always looking for connections and relationships, so draw on this tendency by presenting new material in the form of a story. Make it colorful, humorous, personally relevant, or even a little rude—it's all easier to remember.

- Though study strategies are important, it's essential to have enough down time so your brain can rest, recuperate, and consolidate the new material it's taken in. It may be worth scheduling study sessions so you can sleep immediately afterward, especially if you tackled challenging material. Alternatively, switch tasks to help you turn off for a while.

- Use the power of chunking to reduce the cognitive load on your brain, i.e. the amount of information it has to work to store. Organize many smaller pieces of information into chunks, which are then more easily recalled. The brain can hold approximately seven pieces of information in the working memory at one time, but a "cheat code" is to fold and nest smaller items so that you're effectively remembering far more than seven. As with other techniques, make sure your chunks make sense and are relevant to you to increase your chances of recall.

- Spaced repetition is the practice of frequent recall to combat forgetting. The trick is to space out repeated exposures over a long period and rehearse little and often, rather than cramming.

- Practice testing and retrieval practice is practice that focuses on active, productive memory—it's about *doing* something with the material, thereby embedding it more solidly.

- Each of these memory techniques is best used in conjunction. The more the merrier—combine them in colorful, creative ways and you increase the neural connections you build and ensure that the memory is firmly stored for later retrieval.

CHAPTER 5: EXAM DAY STRATEGIES

- Just as you need a strategy to tackle your exam schedule, you need one to tackle the exam itself on D Day. No two students will have the same strategy, but a good rule of thumb is to make sure you're prepared well ahead of time and that you make your first duty in the exam to read thoroughly and orient yourself before answering anything. Read the paper well to see what you know and which questions will be difficult.
- Before starting, budget your time carefully, taking into account any tricky areas as well as the mark allocation. Note down a mini-schedule and keep an eye on the time to make sure you're sticking to it. Then begin the paper.
- For technical or scientific exams, watch out for units or muddled terms. For other topics, make sure you're taking the time to plan out answers, keeping

organized, and really read what you are being asked in the question.

- Multiple choice questions are easily done with the right strategy. As always, start by reading the questions thoroughly, then try to answer on your own before reading the options. Use a process of elimination to delete obviously wrong answers, then work to discern between two or more very similar answers. Make your decision before a final check right at the end, but resist changing your answer at the last minute. At the very least, you have some non-zero chance of getting it right by accident!

- For essays, most of your success will come down to adequate prep beforehand. Start by anticipating the form and content of the essay question so you can prepare, and then get to work structuring and organizing material so you are ready to answer a range of possible questions. Create outlines for model answers and choose a few to write from scratch under exam conditions.

- Finally, learning doesn't stop after the exam is done. Use your results to help you identify where you've gone wrong, and feed that back into your strategy going forward. This is the essence of learning. Ask what type of error you've made, and commit to addressing it the next time round.